SOFT POWER

The Means to Success in World Politics

JOSEPH S. NYE, JR.

PublicAffairs

New York

Book design by Jane Raese
Text set in 11-point Janson

Library of Congress Cataloging-in-Publication Data
Nye, Jr., Joseph S.
Soft power: the means to success in world politics /
Nye, Jr., Joseph S.—1st ed.
p. cm.
Includes bibliographical references and index.
ISBN-13 978-1-58648-306-7 (pbk)
ISBN-10 1-58648-306-4 (pbk)
1. United States—Foreign relations—Philosophy.
2. Power (Social sciences)—United States.
3. United States—Foreign relations—2001– .
4. World politics—1989–
I. Title.
JZ1480.N94 2004
327.73—dc22
2003069016

20 19 18 17 16

JOSEPH S. NYE JR., former dean of the Kennedy School of Government at Harvard University, was Chairman of the National Intelligence Council and an Assistant Secretary of Defense in the Clinton administration. He is the author of several works of nonfiction, including *The Paradox of American Power* and *Bound to Lead* as well as one novel, *The Power Game*.

ALSO BY JOSEPH S. NYE, JR.

The Paradox of American Power:
Why the World's Only Super Power Can't Go It Alone (2002)

Understanding International Conflicts:
An Introduction to Theory and History, 4th ed. (2002)

Bound to Lead: The Changing Nature of American Power (1990)

Nuclear Ethics (1986)

Hawks, Doves and Owls: An Agenda for Avoiding Nuclear War,
coauthored with Graham Allison and Albert Carnesale (1985)

Power and Interdependence: World Politics in Transition,
coauthored with Robert O. Keohane (1977;
3rd ed. with additional material, 2000)

Peace in Parts: Integration and Conflict
in Regional Organization (1971)

Pan Africanism and East African Integration (1965)

For my mother, Else,
and my sisters, Deb, Naut, and Ellie

Contents

Preface

In 2003, I was sitting in the audience at the World Economic Forum in Davos, Switzerland, when George Carey, former Archbishop of Canterbury, asked Secretary of State Colin Powell why the United States seemed to focus only on its hard power rather than its soft power. I was interested in the question because I had coined the term "soft power" a decade or so earlier. Secretary Powell correctly replied that the United States needed hard power to win World War II, but he continued, "And what followed immediately after hard power? Did the United States ask for dominion over a single nation in Europe? No. Soft power came in the Marshall Plan. . . . We did the same thing in Japan."[1] Later in the same year, I spoke about soft power to a conference cosponsored by the U.S. Army in Washington. One of the other speakers was Secretary of Defense Donald Rumsfeld. According to a press account, "The top military brass listened sympathetically" to my views, but when someone in the audience later asked Rumsfeld for his opinion on soft power, he replied "I don't know what it means."[2]

That is part of our problem. Some of our leaders do not understand the crucial importance of soft power in our reordered post–September 11 world. As former House Speaker Newt Gingrich observed about the Bush administration's approach in Iraq, "The real key is not how many enemy do I kill. The real key is how many allies do I grow. And that is a very important metric that they just don't get."[3] One of Rumsfeld's "rules" is that "weakness is provocative."[4] He is correct up to a point, and as a former assistant secretary of defense, I would be the last person to deny the importance of maintaining our military strength. As Osama bin Laden observed, people like a strong horse. But power comes in many guises, and soft power is not weakness. It is a form of power, and the failure to incorporate it in our national strategy is a serious mistake.

What is soft power? It is the ability to get what you want through attraction rather than coercion or payments. It arises from the attractiveness of a country's culture, political ideals, and policies. When our policies are seen as legitimate in the eyes of others, our soft power is enhanced. America has long had a great deal of soft power. Think of the impact of Franklin Roosevelt's Four Freedoms in Europe at the end of World War II; of young people behind the Iron Curtain listening to American music and news on Radio Free Europe; of Chinese students symbolizing their protests in Tiananmen Square by creating a replica of the Statue of Liberty; of newly liberated Afghans in 2001 asking for a copy of the Bill of Rights; of young Iranians today surreptitiously watching banned American videos and satellite television broadcasts in the privacy of their homes. These are all examples of America's soft power. When you can get others to admire your ideals and to want what you want, you do not have to spend as much on sticks and carrots to move them in your direction. Seduction is always more effective than coercion, and many values like democracy, human rights, and individual opportunities are deeply seductive. As General Wesley Clark put it, soft power "gave us an influence far beyond the hard edge of traditional balance-of-power politics."[5] But attraction can turn to repulsion if we act in an arrogant manner and destroy the real message of our deeper values.

The United States may be more powerful than any other polity since the Roman Empire, but like Rome, America is neither invincible nor invulnerable. Rome did not succumb to the rise of another empire, but to the onslaught of waves of barbarians. Modern high-tech terrorists are the new barbarians. As the world wends its way deeper into a struggle with terrorism, it becomes increasingly apparent that many factors lie outside American control. The United

States cannot alone hunt down every suspected Al Qaeda leader hiding in remote regions of the globe. Nor can it launch a war whenever it wishes without alienating other countries and losing the cooperation it needs for winning the peace.

The four-week war in Iraq in the spring of 2003 was a dazzling display of America's hard military power that removed a tyrant, but it did not resolve our vulnerability to terrorism. It was also costly in terms of our soft power—our ability to attract others to our side. In the aftermath of the war, polling by the Pew Research Center showed a dramatic decline in the popularity of the United States compared to a year earlier, even in countries like Spain and Italy, whose governments had provided support for the war effort, and America's standing plummeted in Islamic countries from Morocco to Turkey to Southeast Asia. Yet the United States will need the help of such countries in the long term to track the flow of terrorists, tainted money, and dangerous weapons. In the words of the *Financial Times*, "To win the peace, therefore, the US will have to show as much skill in exercising soft power as it has in using hard power to win the war."[6]

I first developed the concept of "soft power" in *Bound to Lead*, a book I published in 1990 that disputed the then-prevalent view that America was in decline. I pointed out that the United States was the strongest nation not only in military and economic power, but also in a third dimension that I called soft power. In the ensuing years, I have been pleased to see the concept enter the public discourse, used by the American secretary of state, the British foreign minister, political leaders, and editorial writers as well as academics around the world. At the same time, however, some have misunderstood it, misused and trivialized it as merely the influence of Coca-Cola, Hollywood, blue jeans, and money. Even more frustrating has been to watch some policy makers ignore the importance of our soft power and make us all pay the price by unnecessarily squandering it.

I returned to soft power in 2001 while writing *The Paradox of American Power*, a book that cautioned against triumphalism, the opposite error from the declinism I had warned against in 1990. I spent a dozen or so pages on soft power, but it was only a small part of a broader argument about multilateralism and foreign policy. Friends and critics urged that if I wanted the term to be properly understood and used in foreign policy, I needed to explore and develop it more fully, and that is the purpose of this book.

This book reflects the fraught international relations that arose before, during, and after the Iraq War. Unlike the 1991 Gulf War, when his father built a broad coalition, George W. Bush decided to attack Iraq in 2003 without a second United Nations resolution and with only a small coalition of supporting countries. In doing so, he escaped the constraints of alliances and institutions that many in his administration chafed under, but he also produced doubts about the legitimacy of our actions, and widespread anxieties about how the United States would use its preponderant power. The sharp drop in the attractiveness of the United States around the world made it difficult to recruit support for the occupation and reconstruction of Iraq. Winning the peace is harder than winning a war, and soft power is essential to winning the peace. Yet the way we went to war in Iraq proved to be as costly for our soft power as it was a stunning victory for our hard power.

Readers who are familiar with my earlier work may properly ask what's new here, beyond a discussion of the Iraq War. The answer is "a lot." They will, of course, find some overlaps, particularly in the first chapter, which lays out the basic concepts. But here I have honed the definition, expanded the examples, used new polling data and historical research, and explored the implications and limits of soft power in ways I had not done in either of my earlier works. The first chapter also adds to my analysis of the changing context of power in international politics, and the reasons why soft power is becoming more important than in the past.

The second chapter examines the sources of American soft power in our culture, in our domestic values and policies, and in the substance and style of our foreign policy. Because Americans are not the only ones with soft power, the third chapter looks at the soft power of other nations and nonstate actors. Chapter 4 examines the practical problems of how to wield soft power through public diplomacy, and the concluding chapter summarizes what it all means for the foreign policy of the United States in the aftermath of the Iraq War.

Americans—and others—face an unprecedented challenge from the dark side of globalization and the privatization of war that has accompanied new technologies. This is properly the focus of our new national security strategy, and is sometimes summarized as a war on terrorism. Like the Cold War, the threats posed by various forms of terrorism will not be resolved quickly, and hard military power will play a vital role. But the U.S. government spends four hundred times more on hard power than on soft power. Like the challenge of the Cold War, this one cannot be met by military power alone. That is why it is so essential that Americans—and others—better understand and apply soft power. Smart power is neither hard nor soft. It is both.

Joseph S. Nye, Jr.
Sandwich, New Hampshire
January 2004

Acknowledgments

WHILE I MAY HAVE INVENTED THE CONCEPT of soft power, this book is not mine alone. I am indebted to a number of people for their contributions. First on any list must be Matthew Kohut, my excellent research assistant who provided valuable ideas and suggestions as well as endless streams of data. He was tireless and imaginative in his efforts. Before going off to graduate school, Alexandra Scacco filled that role with equal vigor and intelligence, and many of her suggestions have made their way into the book. Neil Rosendorf, her predecessor, did not work directly on this book, but he helped to introduce me to the history of cultural diplomacy and certainly influenced chapters 2 and 4. I am blessed to have had the privilege of working with these wonderful younger colleagues.

The cooperation of a number of individuals greatly simplified the research tasks. Andrew Kohut and Nicole Speulda at the Pew Research Center provided invaluable assistance with their data. Sally Kuisel at the National Archives, Susan N'Garim and Erin Carriere at the State Department, and the Harvard University research librarians Suzanne Wones, Julie Revak, and Carla Lillvik all made notable contributions.

I am also deeply grateful to my colleagues at the Kennedy School of Government who have provided such a supportive intellectual environment for the analysis of policy over the years. I have drawn a number of ideas from discussions in the multiyear faculty study group on Visions of Governance for the Twenty-first Century. Special help in the form of valuable comments on draft chapters came from Graham Allison, Mark Moore, John Ruggie, Stephen Walt, and Joan Goodman Williamson. Other friends, former students, and family who provided valuable assistance included Kurt Campbell, Fen Hampson, Stanley Hoffmann, Ann Hollick, Peter Feaver, Ben Nye, and Stephen Yetiv. A special category must be reserved for Robert Keohane, my close friend and collaborator for more than three decades. Not only has he provided careful criticism of the draft chapters, but also I have learned so much from our coauthorships and conversations over the years that I should grant him one unending footnote for everything I write. And I am grateful to Kate Darnton for a fine job of intelligent and sensitive editing.

As always, my deepest debt is to Molly Harding Nye, a woman with wondrous soft power.

CHAPTER ONE

The Changing Nature of Power

M ORE THAN FOUR CENTURIES AGO, Niccolo Machiavelli advised princes in Italy that it was more important to be feared than to be loved. But in today's world, it is best to be both. Winning hearts and minds has always been important, but it is even more so in a global information age. Information is power, and modern information technology is spreading information more widely than ever before in history. Yet political leaders have spent little time thinking about how the nature of power has changed and, more specifically, about how to incorporate the soft dimensions into their strategies for wielding power.

WHAT IS POWER?

Power is like the weather. Everyone depends on it and talks about it, but few understand it. Just as farmers and meteorologists try to forecast the weather, political leaders and analysts try to describe and predict changes in power relationships. Power is also like love, easier to experience than to define or measure, but no less real for that. The dictionary tells us that power is the capacity to do things. At this most general level, power means the ability to get the outcomes one wants. The dictionary also tells us that power means having the capabilities to affect the behavior of others to make those things happen. So more specifically, power is the ability to influence the behavior of others to get the outcomes one wants. But there are several ways to affect the behavior of others. You can coerce them with threats; you can induce them with payments; or you can attract and co-opt them to want what you want.

Some people think of power narrowly, in terms of command and coercion. You experience it when you can make others do what they would otherwise not do.[1] You say "Jump!" and they jump. This appears to be a simple test of power, but things are not as straightforward as they first appear. Suppose those whom you command, like my granddaughters, already love to jump? When we measure power in terms of the changed behavior of others, we have first to know their preferences. Otherwise we may be as mistaken about our power as a rooster who thinks his crowing makes the sun rise. And the power may evaporate when the context changes. The playground bully who terrorizes other children and makes them jump at his command loses his power as soon as the class returns from recess to a strict classroom. A cruel dictator can lock up or execute a dissident, but that may not prove his power if the dissenter was really seeking martyrdom. Power always depends on the context in which the relationship exists.[2]

Knowing in advance how others would behave in the absence of our commands is often difficult. What is more, as we shall see, sometimes we can get the outcomes we want by affecting behavior without commanding it. If you believe that my objectives are legitimate, I may be able to persuade you to do something for me without using threats or inducements. It is possible to get many desired outcomes without having much tangible power over others. For example, some loyal Catholics may follow the pope's teaching on capital punishment not because of a threat of excommunication but out of respect for his moral authority. Or some radical Muslim fundamentalists may be attracted to support Osama bin Laden's actions not because of payments or threats, but because they believe in the legitimacy of his objectives.

Practical politicians and ordinary people often find these questions of behavior and motivation too complicated. Thus they turn to a second definition of power and simply define it as the possession of capabilities or resources that can influence outcomes. Consequently they consider a country powerful if it has a relatively large population and territory, extensive natural resources, economic strength, military force, and social stability. The virtue of this second definition is that it makes power appear more concrete, measurable, and predictable. But this definition also has problems. When people define power as synonymous with the resources that produce it, they sometimes encounter the paradox that those best endowed with power do not always get the outcomes they want.

Power resources are not as fungible as money. What wins in one game may not help at all in another. Holding a winning poker hand does not help if the game is bridge.[3] Even if the game is poker, if you play your high hand poorly, you can still lose. Having power resources does not guarantee that you will always get the outcome you want. For example, in terms of resources the United States was far more powerful than Vietnam, yet we lost the Vietnam War. And America was the world's only superpower in 2001, but we failed to prevent September 11.

Converting resources into realized power in the sense of obtaining desired outcomes requires well-designed strategies and skillful leadership. Yet strategies are often inadequate and leaders frequently misjudge—witness Japan and Germany in 1941 or Saddam Hussein in 1990. As a first approximation in any game, it always helps to start by figuring out who is holding the high cards. But it is equally important to understand what game you are playing. Which resources provide the best basis for power behavior in a particular context? Oil was not an impressive power resource before the industrial age nor was uranium significant before the nuclear age.

In earlier periods, international power resources may have been easier to assess. A traditional test of a Great Power in international politics was "strength for war."[4] But over the centuries, as technologies evolved, the sources of strength for war often changed. For example, in eighteenth-century Europe, population was a critical power resource because it provided a base for taxes and the recruitment of infantry. At the end of the Napoleonic Wars in 1815, Prussia presented its fellow victors at the Congress of Vienna with a precise plan for its own reconstruction with territories and populations to be transferred to maintain a balance of power against France. In the prenationalist period, it did not matter that many of the people in those transferred provinces did not speak German. However, within half a century popular sentiments of nationalism had grown greatly, and Germany's seizure of Alsace and Lorraine from France in 1870 became one of the underlying causes of World War I. Instead of being assets, the transferred provinces became liabilities in the changed context of nationalism. In short, power resources cannot be judged without knowing the context. Before you judge who is holding the high cards, you need to understand what game you are playing and how the value of the cards may be changing.

For example, the distribution of power resources in the contemporary information age varies greatly on different issues. We are told that the United States is the only superpower in a "unipolar" world. But the context is far more complex than first meets the eye. The agenda of world politics has become like a three-dimensional chess game in which one can win only by playing vertically as well as horizontally. On the top board of classic interstate military issues, the United States is indeed the only superpower with global military reach, and it makes sense to speak in traditional terms of unipolarity or hegemony. However, on the middle board of interstate economic issues, the distribution of power is multipolar. The United States cannot obtain the outcomes it wants on trade, antitrust, or financial regulation issues without the agreement of the European Union, Japan, China, and others. It makes little sense to call this American hegemony. And on the bottom board of transnational issues like terrorism, international crime, climate change, and the spread of infectious diseases, power is widely distributed and chaotically organized among state and nonstate actors. It makes no sense at all to call this a unipolar world or an American empire—despite the claims of propagandists on the right and left. And this is the set of issues that is now intruding into the world of grand strategy. Yet many political leaders still focus almost entirely on military assets and classic military solutions—the top board. They mistake the necessary for the sufficient. They are one-dimensional players in a three-dimensional game. In the long term, that is the way to lose, since obtaining favorable outcomes on the bottom transnational board often requires the use of soft power assets.

SOFT POWER

Everyone is familiar with hard power. We know that military and economic might often get others to change their position. Hard power can rest on inducements ("carrots") or threats ("sticks"). But sometimes you can get the outcomes you want without tangible threats or payoffs. The indirect way to get what you want has sometimes been called "the second face of power." A country may obtain the outcomes it wants in world politics because other countries—admiring its values, emulating its example, aspiring to its level of prosperity and openness—want to follow it. In this sense, it is also important to set the agenda and attract others in world politics, and not only to force them to change by threatening military force or economic sanctions. This soft power—getting others to want the outcomes that you want—co-opts people rather than coerces them.[5]

Soft power rests on the ability to shape the preferences of others. At the personal level, we are all familiar with the power of attraction and seduction. In a relationship or a marriage, power does not necessarily reside with the larger partner, but in the mysterious chemistry of attraction. And in the business world, smart executives know that leadership is not just a matter of issuing commands, but also involves leading by example and attracting others to do what you want. It is difficult to run a large organization by commands alone. You also need to get others to buy in to your values. Similarly, contemporary practices of community-based policing rely on making the police sufficiently friendly and attractive that a community wants to help them achieve shared objectives.[6]

Political leaders have long understood the power that comes from attraction. If I can get you to want to do what I want, then I do not have to use carrots or sticks to make you do it. Whereas leaders in authoritarian countries can use coercion and issue commands, politicians in democracies have to rely more on a combination of inducement and attraction. Soft power is a staple of daily democratic politics. The ability to establish preferences tends to be associated with intangible assets such as an attractive personality, culture, political values and institutions, and policies that are seen as legitimate or having moral authority. If a leader represents values that others want to follow, it will cost less to lead.

Soft power is not merely the same as influence. After all, influence can also rest on the hard power of threats or payments. And soft power is more than just persuasion or the ability to move people by argument, though that is an important part of it. It is also the ability to attract, and attraction often leads to acquiescence. Simply put, in behavioral terms soft power is attractive power. In terms of resources, soft-power resources are the assets that produce such attraction. Whether a particular asset is a soft-power resource that produces attraction can be measured by asking people through polls or focus groups. Whether that attraction in turn produces desired policy outcomes has to be judged in particular cases. Attraction does not always determine others' preferences, but this gap between power measured as resources and power judged as the outcomes of behavior is not unique to soft power. It occurs with all forms of power. Before the fall of France in 1940, Britain and France had more tanks than Germany, but that advantage in military power resources did not accurately predict the outcome of the battle.

One way to think about the difference between hard and soft power is to consider the variety of ways you can obtain the outcomes you want. You can command me to change my preferences and do what you want by threatening me with force or economic sanctions. You can induce me to do what you want by using your economic power to pay me. You can restrict my preferences by setting the agenda in such a way that my more extravagant wishes seem too unrealistic to pursue. Or you can appeal to a sense of attraction, love, or duty in our relationship and appeal to our shared values about the justness of contributing to those shared values and purposes.[7] If I am persuaded to go along with your purposes without any explicit threat or exchange taking place—in short, if my behavior is determined by an observable but intangible attraction—soft power is at work. Soft power uses a different type of currency (not force, not money) to engender cooperation—an attraction to shared values and the justness and duty of contributing to the achievement of those values. Much as Adam Smith observed that people are led by an invisible hand when making decisions in a free market, our decisions in the marketplace for ideas are often shaped by soft power—an intangible attraction that persuades us to go along with others' purposes without any explicit threat or exchange taking place.

Hard and soft power are related because they are both aspects of the ability to achieve one's purpose by affecting the behavior of others. The distinction between them is one of degree, both in the nature of the behavior and in the tangibility of the resources. Command power—the ability to change what others do—can rest on coercion or inducement. Co-optive power—the ability to shape what others want—can rest on the attractiveness of one's culture and values or the ability to manipulate the agenda of political choices in a manner that makes others fail to express some preferences because they seem to be too unrealistic. The types of behavior between command and co-option range along a spectrum from coercion to economic inducement to agenda setting to pure attraction. Soft-power resources tend to be associated with the co-optive end of the spectrum of behavior, whereas hard-power resources are usually associated with command behavior. But the relationship is imperfect. For example, sometimes countries may be attracted to others with command power by myths of invincibility, and command power may sometimes be used to establish institutions that later become regarded as legitimate. A strong economy not only provides resources for sanctions and payments, but can also be a source of attractiveness. On the whole, however, the general association between the types of behavior and certain resources is strong enough to allow us to employ the useful shorthand reference to hard- and soft-power resources.[8]

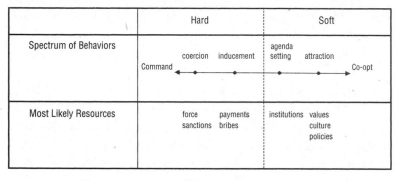

	Hard	Soft
Spectrum of Behaviors	coercion inducement	agenda setting attraction
	Command ◄————————►	————————► Co-opt
Most Likely Resources	force payments sanctions bribes	institutions values culture policies

Power

In international politics, the resources that produce soft power arise in large part from the values an organization or country expresses in its culture, in the examples it sets by its internal practices and policies, and in the way it handles its relations with others. Governments sometimes find it difficult to control and employ soft power, but that does not diminish its importance. It was a former French foreign minister who observed that the Americans are powerful because they can "inspire the dreams and desires of others, thanks to the mastery of global images through film and television and because, for these same reasons, large numbers of students from other countries come to the United States to finish their studies."[9] Soft power is an important reality. Even the great British realist E. H. Carr, writing in 1939, described international power in three categories: military, economic, and power over opinion.[10] Those who deny the importance of soft power are like people who do not understand the power of seduction.

During a meeting with President John F. Kennedy, the senior statesman John J. McCloy exploded in anger about paying attention to popularity and attraction in world politics: "'World opinion'? I don't believe in world opinion. The only thing that matters is power." But like Woodrow Wilson and Franklin Roosevelt, Kennedy understood that the ability to attract others and move opinion was an element of power.[11] He understood the importance of soft power.

As mentioned above, sometimes the same power resources can affect the entire spectrum of behavior from coercion to attraction. A country that suffers economic and military decline is likely to lose not only its hard-power resources but also some of its ability to shape the international agenda and some of its attractiveness. Some countries may be attracted to others with hard power by the myth of invincibility or inevitability. Both Hitler and Stalin tried to develop such myths. Hard power can also be used to establish empires and institutions that set the agenda for smaller states—witness Soviet rule over the countries of Eastern Europe. President Kennedy was properly concerned that although polls showed the United States to be more popular, they also showed a Soviet lead in perceptions of its space program and the strength of its nuclear arsenal.[12]

But soft power does not depend on hard power. The Vatican has soft power despite Stalin's mocking question "How many divisions does the Pope have?" The Soviet Union once had a good deal of soft power, but it lost much of it after the invasions of Hungary and Czechoslovakia. Soviet soft power declined even as its hard economic and military resources continued to grow. Because of its brutal policies, the Soviet Union's hard power actually undercut its soft power. In contrast, the Soviet sphere of influence in Finland was reinforced by a degree of soft power. Similarly, the United States' sphere of influence in Latin America in the 1930s was reinforced when Franklin Roosevelt added the soft power of his "good neighbor policy."[13]

Sometimes countries enjoy political clout that is greater than their military and economic weight would suggest because they define their national interest to include attractive causes such as economic aid or peacemaking. For example, in the past two decades

Norway has taken a hand in peace talks in the Philippines, the Balkans, Colombia, Guatemala, Sri Lanka, and the Middle East. Norwegians say this grows out of their Lutheran missionary heritage, but at the same time the posture of peacemaker identifies Norway with values shared by other nations that enhance Norway's soft power. Foreign Minister Jan Peterson argued that "we gain some access," explaining that Norway's place at so many negotiating tables elevates its usefulness and value to larger countries.[14]

Michael Ignatieff describes the position of Canada from a similar point of view: "Influence derives from three assets: moral authority as a good citizen which we have got some of, military capacity which we have got a lot less of, and international assistance capability." With regard to the United States, "we have something they want. They need legitimacy."[15] That in turn can increase Canada's influence when it bargains with its giant neighbor. The Polish government decided to send troops to postwar Iraq not only to curry favor with the United States but also as a way to create a broader positive image of Poland in world affairs. When the Taliban government fell in Afghanistan in 2001, the Indian foreign minister flew to Kabul to welcome the new interim government in a plane not packed with arms or food but crammed with tapes of Bollywood movies and music, which were quickly distributed across the city.[16] As we shall see in chapter 3, many countries have soft-power resources.

Institutions can enhance a country's soft power. For example, Britain in the nineteenth century and the United States in the second half of the twentieth century advanced their values by creating a structure of international rules and institutions that were consistent with the liberal and democratic nature of the British and American economic systems: free trade and the gold standard in the case of Britain; the International Monetary Fund, the World Trade Organization, and the United Nations in the case of the United States. When countries make their power legitimate in the eyes of others, they encounter less resistance to their wishes. If a country's culture and ideology are attractive, others more willingly follow. If a country can shape international rules that are consistent with its interests and values, its actions will more likely appear legitimate in the eyes of others. If it uses institutions and follows rules that encourage other countries to channel or limit their activities in ways it prefers, it will not need as many costly carrots and sticks.

SOURCES OF SOFT POWER

The soft power of a country rests primarily on three resources: its culture (in places where it is attractive to others), its political values (when it lives up to them at home and abroad), and its foreign policies (when they are seen as legitimate and having moral authority.)

Let's start with culture. Culture is the set of values and practices that create meaning for a society. It has many manifestations. It is common to distinguish between high culture such as literature, art, and education, which appeals to elites, and popular culture, which focuses on mass entertainment.

When a country's culture includes universal values and its policies promote values and interests that others share, it increases the probability of obtaining its desired outcomes because of the relationships of attraction and duty that it creates. Narrow values and parochial cultures are less likely to produce soft power. The United States benefits from a universalistic culture. The German editor Josef Joffe once argued that America's soft power was even larger than its economic and military assets. "U.S. culture, low-brow or high, radiates outward with an intensity last seen in the days of the Roman Empire—but with a novel twist. Rome's and Soviet Russia's cultural sway stopped exactly at their military borders. America's soft power, though, rules over an empire on which the sun never sets."[17]

Some analysts treat soft power simply as popular cultural power. They make the mistake of equating soft power behavior with the cultural resources that sometimes help produce it. They confuse the cultural resources with the behavior of attraction. For example, the historian Niall Ferguson describes soft power as "nontraditional forces such as cultural and commercial goods" and then dismisses it on the grounds "that it's, well, soft."[18] Of course, Coke and Big Macs do not necessarily attract people in the Islamic world to love the United States. The North Korean dictator Kim Jong Il is alleged to like pizza and American videos, but that does not affect his nuclear programs. Excellent wines and cheeses do not guarantee attraction to France, nor does the popularity of Pokémon games assure that Japan will get the policy outcomes it wishes.

This is not to deny that popular culture is often a resource that produces soft power, but as we saw earlier, the effectiveness of any power resource depends on the context. Tanks are not a great military power resource in swamps or jungles. Coal and steel are not major power resources if a country lacks an industrial base. Serbs eating at McDonald's supported Milosevic, and Rwandans committed atrocities while wearing T-shirts with American logos. American films that make the United States attractive in China or Latin America may have the opposite effect and actually reduce American soft power in Saudi Arabia or Pakistan. But in general, polls show that our popular culture has made the United States seem to others "exciting, exotic, rich, powerful, trend-setting—the cutting edge of modernity and innovation."[19] And such images have appeal "in an age when people want to partake of the good life American-style, even if as political citizens, they are aware of the downside for ecology, community, and equality."[20] For example, in explaining a new movement toward using lawsuits to assert rights in China, a young Chinese activist explained, "We've seen a lot of Hollywood movies—they feature weddings, funerals and going to court. So now we think it's only natural to go to court a few times in your life."[21] If American objectives include the strengthening of the legal system in China, such films may be more effective than speeches by the American ambassador about the importance of the rule of law.

As we will see in the next chapter, the background attraction (and repulsion) of American popular culture in different regions and among different groups may make it easier or more difficult for American officials to promote their policies. In some cases, such as

Iran, the same Hollywood images that repel the ruling mullahs may be attractive to the younger generation. In China, the attraction and rejection of American culture among different groups may cancel each other out.

Commerce is only one of the ways in which culture is transmitted. It also occurs through personal contacts, visits, and exchanges. The ideas and values that America exports in the minds of more than half a million foreign students who study every year in American universities and then return to their home countries, or in the minds of the Asian entrepreneurs who return home after succeeding in Silicon Valley, tend to reach elites with power. Most of China's leaders have a son or daughter educated in the States who can portray a realistic view of the United States that is often at odds with the caricatures in official Chinese propaganda. Similarly, when the United States was trying to persuade President Musharraf of Pakistan to change his policies and be more supportive of American measures in Afghanistan, it probably helped that he could hear from a son working in the Boston area.

Government policies at home and abroad are another potential source of soft power. For example, in the 1950s racial segregation at home undercut American soft power in Africa, and today the practice of capital punishment and weak gun control laws undercut American soft power in Europe. Similarly, foreign policies strongly affect soft power. Jimmy Carter's human rights policies are a case in point, as were government efforts to promote democracy in the Reagan and Clinton administrations. In Argentina, American human rights policies that were rejected by the military government of the 1970s produced considerable soft power for the United States two decades later, when the Peronists who were earlier imprisoned subsequently came to power. Policies can have long-term as well as short-term effects that vary as the context changes. The popularity of the United States in Argentina in the early 1990s reflected Carter's policies of the 1970s, and it led the Argentine government to support American policies in the UN and in the Balkans.

Nonetheless, American soft power eroded significantly after the context changed again later in the decade when the United States failed to rescue the Argentine economy from its collapse.

Government policies can reinforce or squander a country's soft power. Domestic or foreign policies that appear to be hypocritical, arrogant, indifferent to the opinion of others, or based on a narrow approach to national interests can undermine soft power. For example, in the steep decline in the attractiveness of the United States as measured by polls taken after the Iraq War in 2003, people with unfavorable views for the most part said they were reacting to the Bush administration and its policies rather than the United States generally. So far, they distinguish American people and culture from American policies. The publics in most nations continued to admire the United States for its technology, music, movies, and television. But large majorities in most countries said they disliked the growing influence of America in their country.[22]

The 2003 Iraq War is not the first policy action that has made the United States unpopular. As we will see in the next chapter, three decades ago, many people around the world objected to America's war in Vietnam, and the standing of the United States reflected the unpopularity of that policy. When the policy changed and the memories of the war receded, the United States recovered much of its lost soft power. Whether the same thing will happen in the aftermath of the Iraq War will depend on the success of policies in Iraq, developments in the Israel-Palestine conflict, and many other factors.

The values a government champions in its behavior at home (for example, democracy), in international institutions (working with others), and in foreign policy (promoting peace and human rights) strongly affect the preferences of others. Governments can attract or repel others by the influence of their example. But soft power does not belong to the government in the same degree that hard power does. Some hard-power assets such as armed forces are strictly governmental; others are inherently national, such as oil and mineral reserves, and many can be transferred to collective control, such as the civilian air fleet that can be mobilized in an emergency. In contrast, many soft-power resources are separate from the American government and are only partly responsive to its purposes. In the Vietnam era, for example, American popular culture often worked at cross-purposes to official government policy. Today, Hollywood movies that show scantily clad women with libertine attitudes or fundamentalist Christian groups that castigate Islam as an evil religion are both (properly) outside the control of government in a liberal society, but they undercut government efforts to improve relations with Islamic nations.

THE LIMITS OF SOFT POWER

Some skeptics object to the idea of soft power because they think of power narrowly in terms of commands or active control. In their view, imitation or attraction are simply that, not power. As we have seen, some imitation or attraction does not produce much power over policy outcomes, and neither does imitation always produce desirable outcomes. For example, in the 1980s, Japan was widely admired for its innovative industrial processes, but imitation by companies in other countries came back to haunt the Japanese when it reduced their market power. Similarly, armies frequently imitate and therefore nullify the successful tactics of their opponents and make it more difficult for them to achieve the outcomes they want. Such observations are correct, but they miss the point that exerting attraction on others often does allow you to get what you want. The skeptics who want to define power only as deliberate acts of command and control are ignoring the second, or "structural," face of power—the ability to get the outcomes you want without having to force people to change their behavior through threats or payments.

At the same time, it is important to specify the conditions under which attraction is more likely to lead to desired outcomes, and under which it will not. As we have seen, popular culture is more likely to attract people and produce soft power in the sense of preferred outcomes in situations where cultures are somewhat similar rather than widely dissimilar. All power depends on context—who relates to whom under what circumstances—but soft power depends more than hard power upon the existence of willing interpreters and receivers. Moreover, attraction often has a diffuse effect, creating general influence rather than producing an easily observable specific action. Just as money can be invested, politicians speak of storing up political capital to be drawn on in future circumstances. Of course, such goodwill may not ultimately be honored, and diffuse reciprocity is less tangible than an immediate exchange. Nonetheless, the indirect effects of attraction and a diffuse influence can make a significant difference in obtaining favorable outcomes in bargaining situations. Otherwise leaders would insist only on immediate payoffs and specific reciprocity, and we know that is not always the way they behave. Social psychologists have developed a substantial body of empirical research exploring the relationship between attractiveness and power.[23]

Soft power is also likely to be more important when power is dispersed in another country rather than concentrated. A dictator cannot be totally indifferent to the views of the people in his country, but he can often ignore whether another country is popular or not when he calculates whether it is in his interests to be helpful. In democracies where public opinion and parliaments matter, political leaders have less leeway to adopt tactics and strike deals than in autocracies. Thus it was impossible for the Turkish government to permit the transport of American troops across the country in 2003 because American policies had greatly reduced our popularity in public opinion and in the parliament. In contrast, it was far easier for the United States to obtain the use of bases in authoritarian Uzbekistan for operations in Afghanistan.

Finally, though soft power sometimes has direct effects on specific goals—witness the inability of the United States to obtain the votes of Chile or Mexico in the UN Security Council in 2003 after our policies reduced our popularity—it is more likely to have an impact on the general goals that a country seeks.[24] Fifty years ago, Arnold Wolfers distinguished between the specific "possession goals" that countries pursue, and their broader "milieu goals," like shaping an environment conducive to democracy.[25] Successful pursuit of both types of goals is important in foreign policy. If one considers various American national interests, for example, soft power may be less relevant than hard power in preventing attack, policing borders, and protecting allies. But soft power is particularly relevant to the realization of "milieu goals." It has a crucial role to play in promoting democracy, human rights, and open markets. It is easier to attract people to democracy than to coerce them to be democratic. The fact that the impact of attraction on achieving preferred outcomes varies by context and type of goals does not make it irrelevant, any more than the fact that bombs and bayonets do not help when we seek to prevent the spread of infectious diseases, slow global warming, or create democracy.

Other skeptics object to using the term "soft power" in international politics because governments are not in full control of the attraction. Much of American soft power has been produced by Hollywood, Harvard, Microsoft, and Michael Jordan. But the fact that civil society is the origin of much soft power does not disprove its existence. In a liberal society, government cannot and should not control the culture. Indeed, the absence of policies of control can itself be a source of attraction. The Czech film director Milos Forman recounts that when the Communist government let in the American film *Twelve Angry Men* because of its harsh portrait of American institutions, Czech intellectuals responded by thinking, "If that country can make this kind of thing, films about itself, oh, that country must have a pride and must have an inner strength, and must be strong enough and must be free."[26]

It is true that firms, universities, foundations, churches, and other nongovernmental groups develop soft power of their own that may reinforce or be at odds with official foreign policy goals. That is all the more reason for governments to make sure that their own actions and policies reinforce rather than undercut their soft power. And this is particularly true since private sources of soft power are likely to become increasingly important in the global information age.

Finally, some skeptics argue that popularity measured by opinion polls is ephemeral and thus not to be taken seriously. Of course, one must be careful not to read too much into opinion polls. They are an essential but imperfect measure of soft-power resources because answers vary depending on the way that questions are formulated, and unless the same questions are asked consistently over some period, they represent snapshots rather than a continuous picture. Opinions can change, and such volatility cannot be captured by any one poll. Moreover, political leaders must often make unpopular decisions because they are the right thing to do, and hope that their popularity may be repaired if the decision is subsequently proved correct. Popularity is not an end in itself in foreign policy. Nonetheless, polls are a good first approximation of both how attractive a country appears and the costs that are incurred by unpopular policies, particularly when they show consistency across polls and over time. And as we shall see in the next chapter, that attractiveness can have an effect on our ability to obtain the outcomes we want in the world.

THE CHANGING ROLE OF
MILITARY POWER

In the twentieth century, science and technology added dramatic new dimensions to power resources. With the advent of the nuclear age, the United States and the Soviet Union possessed not only industrial might but nuclear arsenals and intercontinental missiles. The age of the superpowers had begun. Subsequently, the leading role of the United States in the information revolution near the end of the century allowed it to create a revolution in military affairs. The ability to use information technology to create precision weapons, real-time intelligence, broad surveillance of regional battlefields, and improved command and control allowed the United States to surge ahead as the world's only military superpower.

But the progress of science and technology had contradictory effects on military power over the past century. On the one hand, it made the United States the world's only superpower, with unmatched military might, but at the same time it gradually increased the political and social costs of using military force for conquest. Paradoxically, nuclear weapons were acceptable for deterrence, but they proved so awesome and destructive that they became musclebound—too costly to use in war except, theoretically, in the most extreme circumstances.[27] Non-nuclear North Vietnam prevailed over nuclear America, and non-nuclear Argentina was not deterred from attacking the British Falkland Islands despite Britain's nuclear status.

A second important change was the way that modern communications technology fomented the rise and spread of nationalism, which made it more difficult for empires to rule over socially awakened populations. In the nineteenth century, Britain ruled a quarter of the globe with a tiny fraction of the world's population. As nationalism grew, colonial rule became too expensive and the British empire collapsed. Formal empires with direct rule over subject populations such as Europe exercised during the nineteenth and twentieth centuries are simply too costly in the twenty-first century.

In addition to nuclear and communications technology, social changes inside the large democracies also raised the costs of using military power. Postindustrial democracies are focused on welfare rather than glory, and they dislike high casualties. This does not mean that they will not use force, even when casualties are expected—witness Britain, France, and the United States in the 1991 Gulf War, and Britain and the United States in the 2003 Iraq War. But the absence of a prevailing warrior ethic in modern democracies means that the use of force requires an elaborate moral justification to ensure popular support, unless actual survival is at stake. For advanced democracies, war remains possible, but it is much less acceptable than it was a century, or even a half century, ago.[28] The most powerful states have lost much of the lust to conquer.[29]

Robert Kagan has correctly pointed out that these social changes have gone further in Europe than the United States, although his clever phrase that Americans are from Mars and Europeans from Venus oversimplifies the differences.[30] After all, Europeans joined in pressing for the use of force in Kosovo in 1999, and the Iraq War demonstrated that there were Europeans from Mars and Americans who preferred Venus. Nonetheless, the success of the European countries in creating an island of peace on the continent that had been ravaged by three Franco-German wars in less than a century may predispose them toward more peaceful solutions to conflict.

However, in a global economy even the United States must consider how the use of force might jeopardize its economic objectives. After its victory in World War II the United States helped to restructure Japan's economy, but it is hard to imagine that the United States today could effectively threaten force to open Japanese markets or change the value of the yen. Nor can one easily imagine the United States using force to resolve disputes with Canada or Europe. Unlike earlier periods, islands of peace where the use of force is no longer an option in relations among states have come to characterize relations among most modern liberal democracies, and not just in Europe. The existence of such islands of peace is evidence of the increasing importance of soft power where there are shared values about what constitutes acceptable behavior among similar democratic states. In their relations with each other, all advanced democracies are from Venus.

Even nondemocratic countries that feel fewer popular moral constraints on the use of force have to consider its effects on their economic objectives. War risks deterring investors who control flows of capital in a globalized economy.[31] A century ago, it may have been easier to seize another state's territory by force than "to develop the sophisticated economic and trading apparatus needed to derive benefit from commercial exchange with it."[32] But it is difficult to imagine a scenario today in which, for example, Japan would try to or succeed in using military force to colonize its neighbors. As two RAND analysts argue, "In the information age, 'cooperative' advantages will become increasingly important. Moreover, societies that improve their abilities to cooperate with friends and allies may also gain competitive advantages against rivals."[33]

None of this is to suggest that military force plays no role in international politics today. On the contrary, the information revolution has yet to transform most of the world, and many states are unconstrained by democratic societal forces. Civil wars are rife in many parts of the world where collapsed empires left failed states and power vacuums. Even more important is the way in which the democratization of technology is leading to the privatization of war. Technology is a double-edged sword. On the one hand, technological and social changes are making war more costly for modern democracies. But at the same time, technology is putting new means of destruction into the hands of extremist groups and individuals.

TERRORISM AND
THE PRIVATIZATION OF WAR

Terrorism is not new, nor is it a single enemy. It is a long-standing method of conflict frequently defined as deliberate attack on noncombatants with the objective of spreading fear and intimidation. Already a century ago, the novelist Joseph Conrad had drawn an indelible portrait of the terrorist mind, and terrorism was a familiar phenomenon in the twentieth century. Whether homegrown or transnational, it was a staple of conflicts throughout the Middle East, in Northern Ireland, Spain, Sri Lanka, Kashmir, South Africa, and elsewhere. It occurred on every continent except Antarctica and affected nearly every country. September 11, 2001, was a dramatic escalation of an age-old phenomenon. Yet two developments have made terrorism more lethal and more difficult to manage in the twenty-first century.

One set of trends grows out of progress in science and technology. First, there is the complex, highly technological nature of modern civilization's basic systems. As a committee of the National Academy of Sciences pointed out, market forces and openness have combined to increase the efficiency of many of our vital systems such as those that provide transportation, information, energy, and health care. But some (though not all) systems become more vulnerable and fragile as they become more complex and efficient.[34]

At the same time, progress is "democratizing technology," making the instruments of mass destruction smaller, cheaper, and more readily available to a far wider range of individuals and groups. Where bombs and timers were once heavy and expensive, plastic explosives and digital timers are light and cheap. The costs of hijacking an airplane are sometimes little more than the price of a ticket.

In addition, the success of the information revolution is providing inexpensive means of communication and organization that allow groups once restricted to local and national police jurisdictions to become global in scope. Thirty years ago, instantaneous global communication was sufficiently expensive that it was restricted to large entities with big budgets like governments, multinational corporations, or the Roman Catholic church. Today the Internet makes global communication virtually free for anyone with access to a modem.[35] Similarly, the Internet has reduced the costs of searching for information and making contacts related to instruments of widescale destruction. Terrorists also depend on getting their messages out quickly to a broad audience through mass media and the Internet—witness the widespread dissemination of bin Laden's television interviews and videotapes after September 11. Terrorism depends crucially on soft power for its ultimate victory. It depends on its ability to attract support from the crowd at least as much as its ability to destroy the enemy's will to fight.

The second set of trends reflects changes in the motivation and organization of terrorist groups. Terrorists in the mid-twentieth century tended to have relatively well-defined political objectives, which were often ill served by mass destruction. They were said to want many people watching rather than many people killed. Such terrorists were often supported and covertly controlled by governments such as Libya or Syria. Toward the end of the century, radical groups grew on the fringes of several religions. Most numerous were the tens of thousands of young Muslim men who went to fight against the Soviet occupation of Afghanistan. There they were trained in a wide range of techniques, and many were recruited to organizations with an extreme view of the religious obligation of jihad. As the historian Walter Laquer has observed, "Traditional terrorists, whether left-wing, right-wing, or nationalist-separatists, were not greatly drawn to these opportunities for greater destruction. . . . Terrorism has become more brutal and indiscriminate since then."[36]

This trend is reinforced when motivations change from narrowly political to unlimited or retributive objectives reinforced by promises of rewards in another world. Fortunately, unlike communism and fascism, Islamist ideology has failed to attract a wide following outside the Islamic community, but that community provides a large pool of over a billion people from which to recruit. Organization has also changed. For example, Al Qaeda's network of thousands of people in loosely affiliated cells in some 60 countries gives it a scale well beyond anything seen before. But even small networks can be more difficult to penetrate than the hierarchical quasi-military organizations of the past.

Both trends, technological and ideological, have created a new set of conditions that have increased both the lethality of terrorism and the difficulty of managing terrorism today. Because of September 11 and the unprecedented scale of Al Qaeda, the current focus is properly on terrorism associated with Islamic extremists. But it would be a mistake to limit our attention or responses to Islamic terrorists, for that would be to ignore the wider effects of the democratization of technology and the broader set of challenges that must be met. Technological progress is putting into the hands of deviant groups and individuals destructive capabilities that were once limited primarily to governments and armies. Every large group of people has some members who deviate from the norm, and some who are bent on destruction. It is worth remembering that the worst terrorist act in the United States before September 11 was the one committed by Timothy McVeigh, a purely homegrown antigovernment fanatic. Similarly, the Aum Shinrykio cult, which released sarin in the Tokyo subway system in 1995, had nothing to do with Islam. Even if the current wave of Islamic terrorism turns out to be generational or cyclical, like terrorist waves in the past, the world will still have to confront the long-term secular dangers arising out of the democratization of technology.

Lethality has been increasing. In the 1970s, the Palestinian attack on Israeli athletes at the Munich Olympics or the killings by the Red Brigades that galvanized world attention cost dozens of lives. In the 1980s, Sikh extremists bombed an Air India flight and killed over 300 people. September 11, 2001, cost several thousand lives—and all of this escalation occurred without the use of weapons of mass destruction. If one extrapolates this lethality trend and imagines a deviant group in some society gaining access to biological or nuclear materials within the coming decade, it is possible to imagine terrorists being able to destroy millions of lives.

In the twentieth century, a pathological individual like Hitler or Stalin or Pol Pot required the apparatus of a totalitarian government to kill large numbers of people. Unfortunately, it is now all too easy to envisage extremist groups and individuals killing millions without the instruments of governments. This is truly the "privatization of war," and it represents a dramatic change in world politics. Moreover, this next step in the escalation of terrorism could have profound effects on the nature of our urban civilization. What will happen to the willingness of people to locate in cities, to our ability to sustain cultural institutions, if instead of destroying two office buildings, a future attack destroys the lower half of Manhattan, the City area of London, or the Left Bank of Paris?

The new terrorism is not like the 1970s terrorism of the IRA, the ETA (the military wing of the Basque separatist movement), or Italy's Red Brigades, nor is the vulnerability limited to any one society. A "business as usual" attitude toward curbing terrorism is not enough. Force still plays a role in world politics, but its nature has changed in the twenty-first century. Technology is increasing terrorists' access to destructive power, but they also benefit greatly from increased capacities to communicate—with each other across jurisdictions, and with global audiences. As we will see in chapter 3, many terrorists groups also have soft as well as hard power. The United States was correct in altering its national security strategy to focus on terrorism and weapons of mass destruction after September 11, 2001. But the means the Bush administration chose focused too heavily on hard power and did not take enough account of soft power. And that is a mistake, because it is through soft power that terrorists gain general support as well as new recruits.

THE INTERPLAY OF
HARD AND SOFT POWER

Hard and soft power sometimes reinforce and sometimes interfere with each other. A country that courts popularity may be loath to exercise its hard power when it should, but a country that throws its weight around without regard to the effects on its soft power may find others placing obstacles in the way of its hard power. No country likes to feel manipulated, even by soft power. At the same time, as mentioned earlier, hard power can create myths of invincibility or inevitability that attract others. In 1961, President John F. Kennedy went ahead with nuclear testing despite negative polls because he worried about global perceptions of Soviet gains in the arms race. Kennedy "was willing to sacrifice some of America's 'soft' prestige in return for gains in the harder currency of military prestige."[37] On a lighter note, it is amusing that in 2003, just a few months after massive antiwar protests in London and Milan, fashion shows in those cities used models in U.S. military commando gear exploding balloons. As one designer put it, American symbols "are still the strongest security blanket."[38]

Throughout history, weaker states have often joined together to balance and limit the power of a stronger state that threatens. But not always. Sometimes the weak are attracted to jumping on the bandwagon led by a strong country, particularly when they have little choice or when the large country's military power is accompanied by soft power. Moreover, as we saw earlier, hard power can some-times have an attractive or soft side. As Osama bin Laden put it in one of his videos, "When people see a strong horse and a weak horse, by nature, they will like the strong horse."[39] And to deliber-ately mix the metaphor, people are more likely to be sympathetic to underdogs than to bet on them.

The 2003 Iraq War provides an interesting example of the inter-play of the two forms of power. Some of the motives for war were based on the deterrent effect of hard power. Donald Rumsfeld is re-ported to have entered office believing that the United States "was seen around the world as a paper tiger, a weak giant that couldn't take a punch" and determined to reverse that reputation.[40] America's military victory in the first Gulf War had helped to produce the Oslo process on Middle East peace, and its 2003 victory in Iraq might eventually have a similar effect. Moreover, states like Syria and Iran might be deterred in their future support of terrorists. These were all hard power reasons to go to war. But another set of motives related to soft power. The neoconservatives believed that American power could be used to export democracy to Iraq and transform the politics of the Middle East. If successful, the war would become self-legitimizing. As William Kristol and Lawrence Kaplan put it, "What is wrong with dominance in the service of sound principles and high ideals?"[41]

Part of the contest about going to war in Iraq became a struggle over the legitimacy of the war. Even when a military balance of power is impossible (as at present, with America the only super-power), other countries can still band together to deprive the U.S. policy of legitimacy and thus weaken American soft power. France, Russia, and China chafed at American military unipolarity and urged a more multipolar world. In Charles Krauthammer's view, Iraq "provided France an opportunity to create the first coherent challenge to that dominance."[42] Even without directly countering the superpower's military power, the weaker states hoped to deter the U.S. by making it more costly for us to use our hard power.[43] They were not able to prevent the United States from going to war, but by depriving the United States of the legitimacy of a second Security Council resolution, they certainly made it more expensive.

Soft balancing was not limited to the UN arena. Outside the UN, diplomacy and peace movements helped transform the global debate from the sins of Saddam to the threat of American empire. That made it difficult for allied countries to provide bases and support and thus cut into American hard power. As noted earlier, the Turkish parliament's refusal to allow transport of ground troops and Saudi Arabia's reluctance to allow American use of air bases that had been available in 1991 are cases in point.

Since the global projection of American military force in the future will require access and overflight rights from other countries, such soft balancing can have real effects on hard power. When support for America becomes a serious vote loser, even friendly leaders are less likely to accede to our requests. In addition, bypassing the UN raised the economic costs to the United States after the war, leading the columnist Fareed Zakaria to observe, "The imperial style of foreign policy is backfiring. At the end of the Iraq war the administration spurned any kind of genuine partnership with the world. It pounded away at the United Nations."[44]

In the summer of 2003, the Bush administration's initial resistance to a significant role for the United Nations in the reconstruction of Iraq is estimated to have cost the United States more than $100 billion, or about $1,000 per American household. In most major peacekeeping missions, the UN covers most of the expenses for countries that contribute troops. In the 1991 Gulf War, the broad coalition assembled by President George H. W. Bush covered 80 percent of the costs, and during the Clinton interventions abroad, the United States shouldered only 15 percent of the reconstruction and peacekeeping costs.[45] But without a UN mandate, some countries refused to participate in peacekeeping in Iraq, and for those who did—countries such as Poland, Ukraine, Nicaragua, El Salvador, Honduras, and others—it was estimated that the United States would have to spend $250 million to help underwrite their participation.[46]

Some neoconservatives argued that the solution was to avoid the UN and to deny its legitimacy. For some, thwarting the UN was a gain.[47] They viewed the Iraq War as a "twofer": it removed Saddam and damaged the UN. Some urged the creation of an alliance of democracies to replace the UN. But such responses ignore the fact that the key divisions were among the democracies, and the United States can influence but not alone determine international views of the legitimacy of the UN. Moreover, soft balancing that puts pressure on parliaments in democracies can be conducted outside the framework of the UN. The Internet has allowed protests to be quickly mobilized by free-wheeling amorphous groups, rather than hierarchical organizations. In the Vietnam era, planning a protest required weeks and months of pamphlets, posters, and phone calls, and it took four years before the size of the protest rallies, 25,000 at first, reached half a million in 1969. In contrast, 800,000 people turned out in the United States and 1.5 million in Europe on one weekend in February 2003 before the start of the war.[48]

Protests do not represent the "international community," but they do often affect the attitudes of editorial writers, parliamentarians, and other influential people in important countries whose views are summarized by that vague phrase.[49] Though the concept of an international community may be imprecise, even those who dismissed international concerns about how the United States entered the war seem to appeal to such opinion when they argue that the legitimacy of American actions will be accepted after the fact if we produce a better Iraq. Such post hoc legitimization may help to restore American soft power that was lost on the way in, but it also shows that legitimacy matters. And in the difficult cases of Iran and North Korea, it is worth noting that President Bush appealed to the views of the "international community" that some of his advisors dismissed as "illusory."[50] The continual contest for legitimacy illustrates the importance of soft power. Morality can be a power reality.

The initial effect of the Iraq War on opinion in the Islamic world was quite negative. Al Jazeera television (the soft-power resource owned by the same government of Qatar that provided headquarters for American hard power) showed bloody pictures of civilian casualties night after night. An Egyptian parliamentarian observed, "You can't imagine how the military strikes on Baghdad and other cities are provoking people every night."[51] In Pakistan, a former diplomat reported that "the US invasion of Iraq is a complete gift to the Islamic parties. People who would otherwise turn up their noses at them are now flocking to their banner."[52] American intelligence and law enforcement officials reported that Al Qaeda and other terrorist groups intensified their recruitment on three continents by "tapping into rising anger about the American campaign for war in Iraq."[53] After the war, polls found a rise in support for bin Laden and a fall in the popularity of the United States even in friendly countries such as Indonesia and Jordan.[54] Meanwhile, in Europe polls showed that the way the United States went about the Iraq War had dissipated the outflow of sympathy and goodwill that had followed the September 11 events. It is still too soon to tell whether the hard-power gains from the war in Iraq will in the long run exceed the soft-power losses, or how permanent the latter will turn out to be, but the war provided a fascinating case study of the interaction of the two types of power.

Looking to the future, much will depend on the effectiveness of American policies in creating a better Iraq and moving the Middle East peace process forward. In addition, much will depend on whether the intelligence failures and political exaggeration of intelligence evidence will have a permanent damaging effect on the credibility of the American government when it approaches other countries for help on cases like Iran and North Korea, as well as in the war on terrorism. As the British weekly *The Economist* observed, "The spies erred and the politicians exaggerated. . . . The war, we think, was justified. But in making the case for it, Mr Bush and Mr Blair did not play straight with their people."[55]

Skeptics argue that because countries cooperate out of self-interest, the loss of soft power does not matter much. But the skeptics miss the point that cooperation is a matter of degree, and that degree is affected by attraction or repulsion. They also miss the point that the effects on nonstate actors and recruitment to terrorist organization do not depend on government attitudes. Already in 2002, well before the Iraq War, reactions against heavy-handed American policies on the Korean peninsula had led to a dramatic drop over the past three years in the percentage of the Korean population favoring an American alliance, from 89 to only 56 percent.[56] That will complicate dealing with the dangerous case of North Korea. Whether in the Middle East or in East Asia, hard and soft power are inextricably intertwined in today's world.

POWER IN A GLOBAL INFORMATION AGE

Power today is less tangible and less coercive among the advanced democracies than it was in the past. At the same time, much of the world does not consist of advanced democracies, and that limits the global transformation of power. For example, most African and the Middle Eastern countries have preindustrial agricultural economies, weak institutions, and authoritarian rulers. Failed states such as Somalia, Congo, Sierra Leone, and Liberia provide venues for violence. Some large countries such as China, India, and Brazil are industrializing and may suffer some of the disruptions that analogous parts of the West encountered at similar stages of their development early in the twentieth century.[57] In such a diverse world, all three sources of power—military, economic, and soft—remain relevant, although in different degrees in different relationships. However, if the current economic and social trends of the information revolution continue, soft power will become more important in the mix.

The information revolution and globalization of the economy are transforming and shrinking the world. At the beginning of the twenty-first century, these two forces have enhanced American power. But with time, technology will spread to other countries and peoples, and America's relative preeminence will diminish. Today Americans represent one twentieth of the global population total, but nearly half of the world's Internet users. Though English may

	Behaviors	Primary Currencies	Government Policies
Military Power	coercion deterrence protection	threats force	coercive diplomacy war alliance
Economic Power	inducement coercion	payments sanctions	aid bribes sanctions
Soft Power	attraction agenda setting	values culture policies institutions	public diplomacy bilateral and multilateral diplomacy

Three Types of Power

remain the lingua franca, as Latin did after the ebb of Rome's might, at some point in the future, perhaps in a decade or two, the Asian cyber-community and economy may loom larger than the American. Even more important, the information revolution is creating virtual communities and networks that cut across national borders. Transnational corporations and nongovernmental actors (terrorists included) will play larger roles. Many of these organizations will have soft power of their own as they attract citizens into coalitions that cut across national boundaries. Politics then becomes in part a competition for attractiveness, legitimacy, and credibility. The ability to share information—and to be believed—becomes an important source of attraction and power.

This political game in a global information age suggests that the relative importance of soft power will increase. The countries that are likely to be more attractive and gain soft power in the information age are those with multiple channels of communication that help to frame issues; whose dominant culture and ideas are closer to prevailing global norms (which now emphasize liberalism, pluralism, and autonomy); and whose credibility is enhanced by their domestic and international values and policies. These conditions suggest opportunities for the United States, but also for Europe and others, as we shall see in chapter 3.

The soft power that is becoming more important in the information age is in part a social and economic by-product rather than solely a result of official government action. Nonprofit institutions with soft power of their own can complicate and obstruct government efforts, and commercial purveyors of popular culture can hinder as well as help the government achieve its objectives. But the larger long-term trends can help the United States if it learns to use them well. To the extent that official policies at home and abroad are consistent with democracy, human rights, openness, and respect for the opinions of others, America will benefit from the trends of this global information age. But there is a danger that the United States may obscure the deeper message of its values through arrogance. As we shall see in the next chapter, American culture high and low still helps produce soft power in the information age, but government actions also matter, not only through programs like the Voice of America and Fulbright scholarships, but, even more important, when policies avoid arrogance and stand for values that others admire. The larger trends of the information age are in America's favor, but only if we learn to stop stepping on our best message. Smart power means learning better how to combine our hard and soft power.

CHAPTER TWO

Sources of
American Soft Power

THE UNITED STATES has many resources that can potentially provide soft power, particularly when one considers the ways in which economic prowess contributes not only to wealth but also to reputation and attractiveness. Not only is America the world's largest economy, but nearly half of the top 500 global companies are American, five times as many as next-ranked Japan.[1] Sixty-two of the top 100 global brands are American, as well as eight of the top ten business schools.[2]

Social indices show a similar pattern. Consider the following:

* The United States attracts nearly six times the inflow of foreign immigrants as second-ranked Germany.[3]
* The United States is far and away the world's number one exporter of films and television programs, although India's "Bollywood" actually produces more movies per year.[4]
* Of the 1.6 million students enrolled in universities outside their own countries, 28 percent are in the United States, compared to the 14 percent who study in Britain.[5]
* More than 86,000 foreign scholars were in residence at American educational institutions in 2002.[6]

Other measures show that the United States . . .

✳ . . . publishes more books than any other country.

✳ . . . has more than twice as many music sales as next-ranked Japan.

✳ . . . has more than 13 times as many Internet website hosts as Japan.

✳ . . . ranks first in Nobel prizes for physics, chemistry, and economics.

✳ . . . places a close second to France for Nobel prizes in literature.

✳ . . . publishes nearly four times as many scientific and journal articles as the next runner-up, Japan.[7]

Of course, the United States does not rank at the top in all measures of potential attraction. According to the 2003 United Nations Development Program's quality-of-life index (which takes into account not only income but also education, health care, and life expectancy), Norway, Iceland, Sweden, Australia, the Netherlands, and Belgium rank ahead of the United States as the best countries in which to live.[8] Japan outranks the U.S. in the number of patents granted to residents and the percentage of GNP it spends on research and development. Britain and Germany rank ahead as havens for asylum seekers. France and Spain attract more tourists than the United States (though the U.S. ranks higher in revenues from tourism). When it comes to "unattractive indicators," the United States ranks near the bottom of the list of rich countries in the level of development assistance it gives, but at the top in the percentage of its population that is incarcerated.[9]

Even more important for power than some high unattractiveness ratings is the fact that, as we saw in the previous chapter, potential power resources do not always translate into realized power in the sense of achieving desired outcomes. For that to happen, the objective measure of potential soft power has to be attractive in the eyes of specific audiences, and that attraction must influence policy outcomes. In this chapter we shall look at several examples of how such attraction has affected important policy outcomes. But first, let's look at some causes of change in the attractiveness of the United States and how that can affect policy outcomes.

THE RISE AND FALL
OF ANTI-AMERICANISM

Despite its impressive resources, the attractiveness of the United States declined quite sharply in 2003. In the run-up to the Iraq War, polls showed that the United States lost an average of 30 points of support in most European countries. Levels of support were even lower in Islamic countries. After the war, majorities of the people held unfavorable images of the United States in nearly two-thirds of 19 countries surveyed. Most of those who held negative views said they blamed the policies of the Bush administration rather than America in general.[10]

Opposition to American policies is not the same as general opposition to the United States. Reactions to policies are more volatile than underlying reactions to culture and values. The image or attractiveness of a country is composed of foreigners' attitudes on a variety of levels and types, of which reactions to American policy constitute only one.

Figure 2.1, which is based on the results of a 2002 poll of 43 countries, indicates the extent to which the United States is admired for its technological and scientific advances as well as its music, movies, and television. At the same time, majorities in 34 of those 43 countries said they disliked the growing influence of America in their country.[11]

The Iraq War was not the first time that a controversial security policy reduced the attractiveness of the American image in other countries. There have been four prior periods when U.S. attractiveness was reduced in Europe: after the 1956 Suez Canal crisis; during the "ban the bomb" movement of the late fifties and early sixties (though this was primarily in Britain and France, not in Germany and Italy); during the Vietnam War era in the late sixties and early

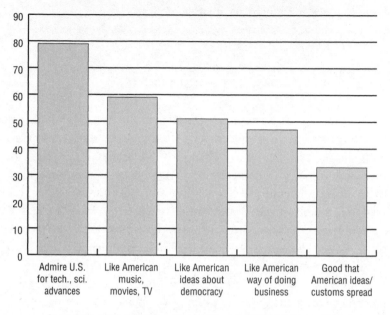

Figure 2.1 Dimensions of American Attractiveness

Source: Pew Global Attitudes Project, *What the World Thinks in 2002.*
Median measures of 43 countries surveyed

seventies; and during the deployment of intermediate-range nuclear weapons in Germany in the early eighties.

The Vietnam War was broadly opposed in Britain, France, Germany, and Italy. Although there was a decline in the overall popularity of the United States from 1965 to 1972 (by about 23 points in Britain, 32 in Germany, 19 in Italy, 7 in France), majorities in all but France continued to express positive opinions of the United States throughout the major operations of the war and right up to the Paris Peace Talks of 1972.[12] Nevertheless, the slide in popularity did have effects on the ability of the American government to achieve its desired policy outcomes. Loss of attractiveness hindered President Lyndon Johnson's efforts to obtain support from other countries for the war in Vietnam, and the drop in soft power hurt other policies as

Figure 2.2 Percentage of Western Europeans Who Say They Have a Very or Somewhat Favorable Opinion of the United States, 1982 to 2003

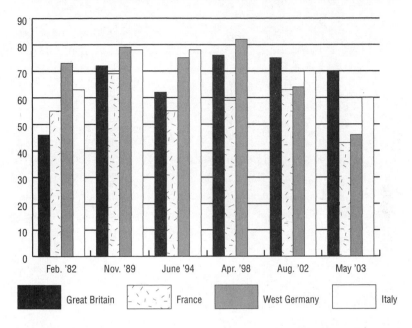

well. In France, for example, Vietnam "contributed to the popular support that sustained de Gaulle's increasingly anti-NATO and anti-U.S. stance."[13]

In the early 1980s, the nuclear weapons policies of the first Reagan Administration aroused considerable concern. In a 1983 *Newsweek* poll, pluralities of around 40 percent of the people polled in France, Britain, Germany, and Japan disapproved of American policies. At the same time, majorities in all those countries approved of the American people.[14] President Reagan was able to get European agreement for deployment of intermediate-range nuclear forces, but there was considerable European resistance to his policy efforts to isolate the Soviet Union economically. Figure 2.2 indicates how over the years the attractiveness of the United States has varied.

Unpopular policies are the most volatile element of the overall image, and there seems to be more stability in the reservoir of goodwill that rests on culture and values.

Nonetheless, there has also been anti-Americanism in the sense of a deeper rejection of American society, values, and culture. It has long been a minor but persistent strand in the image, and it goes back to the earliest days of the republic, when Europeans turned America into a symbol in their own internal culture wars. Already in the eighteenth century, some Europeans were absurdly arguing that the excessive humidity in the New World led to degenerate forms of life.[15] Although some nineteenth-century Europeans saw America as a symbol of freedom, others, such as the author Charles Dickens, saw only "a clamorous gang of fakes, fools, and tricksters."[16] In the early twentieth century, even as sensitive a writer as Virginia Woolf treated America with a mixture of disdain and disinterest. For many on the European Left, America was a symbol of capitalist exploitation of the working class, while those on the right saw it as degenerate because of its racial impurity.[17]

Some conservatives disliked the egalitarian nature of American popular culture. In 1931, a former viceroy of India complained to Conservative MPs that Hollywood had helped to shatter "the white man's prestige in the East," and Belgium banned Africans in its colony the Congo from attending American films.[18] Even today, as the London-based *Economist* points out, anti-Americanism is partly a class issue: "Poorer and less-educated Britons like America a lot more than their richer compatriots. . . . Upper class anti-Americanism may be surrogate snobbery."[19] Intellectual snobbery should be added to the list. European elites have always grumbled about America's lack of sophistication, but polls show that America's pop culture resonates widely with the majority of the people across the continent.

Another source of anti-Americanism is structural. The United States is the big kid on the block and the disproportion in power engenders a mixture of admiration, envy, and resentment. Indeed, as the United States emerged as a global power at the beginning of the twentieth century, a British author, W. T. Stead, had already written a book called *The Americanization of the World*, published in 1902. Similarly, in the mid-1970s majorities across Western Europe told pollsters they preferred an equal distribution of power between the United States and the USSR rather than U.S. dominance.[20] But those who dismiss the recent rise of anti-Americanism as simply the inevitable result of size are mistaken in thinking nothing can be done about it.

Policies can soften or sharpen hard structural edges, and they can affect the ratio of love to hate in complex love-hate relationships. The United States was even more preeminent than now at the end of World War II, when it represented more than a third of the world economy and was the only country with nuclear weapons, but it pursued policies that were acclaimed by allied countries. Similarly, American leadership was welcome to many even when the end of the Cold War meant there was no longer any country that could balance American power. For example, the Yugoslav intellectual Milovan Djilas argued in 1992 that if the power of the U.S. weakened, "then the way is open to everything bad." And on the other side of the world, in 1990, Naohiro Amaya, a high official in a then-buoyant Japan, said, "Whether we like it or not, there will be no free world and no free trading system if the U.S. does not preserve them for us. The best Japan can aspire to is 'vice president.'"[21] Size may create a love-hate relationship, but since in recent decades size is a constant, it cannot explain why anti-Americanism is higher or lower at some times than at others.

In addition to its size, the United States has long stood for modernity, which some people regard as threatening to their cultures. In the nineteenth century, Europeans on the Right who resisted industrial society and those on the Left who wanted to reshape it pointed with fear or scorn at America. A similar phenomenon is true today with the growth of globalization. In some areas, there is not only a resentment of American cultural imports, but also of American culture itself. Polls in 2002 found that majorities in 34 of 43 countries agreed with the statement "It's bad that American ideas and customs are spreading here."[22]

It is probably inevitable that those who resent American power and the cultural impact of economic globalization confuse the two and use nationalism to resist both. Jose Bové, a French sheep farmer, earned fame by destroying a McDonald's restaurant in his local region in France.[23] No one forces people to eat at McDonald's, but Bové's ability to attract global media attention reflects the cultural ambivalence toward things American. As Iran's president complained in 1999, "The new world order and globalization that certain powers are trying to make us accept, in which the culture of the entire world is ignored, looks like a kind of neocolonialism."[24] A writer for the German magazine *Der Spiegel* commented that it is time to fight back "before the entire world wears a Made in USA label."[25]

It is much too simple to equate globalization with Americanization. Other cultures contribute mightily to global connections. English, the lingua franca of modern commerce, was originally spread by Britain, not the United States.[26] As we will see in the next chapter, the globally significant ties between French-, Spanish-, and Portuguese-speaking countries, respectively, have nothing to do with the United States. AIDS originated in Africa and SARS in Asia. Soccer is far more popular internationally than American football. The most popular sports team in the world is not American: it is Britain's soccer behemoth, Manchester United, with 200 fan clubs in 24 countries. The global stardom of the player David Beckham was such that he was able to carry it with him after he was traded to the Madrid club. The Beatles and Rolling Stones were imports to America. Three of the leading "American" music labels have British, German, and Japanese owners. Japan leads in the creation of animation and the most popular video games around the world.[27] The rise of reality programming in television entertainment in recent years spread from Europe to the United States, not vice versa. Even McDonald's is drawing lessons from France for the redesign of some of its American restaurants.[28] Globalization's contours are not solely American, though quite naturally its current effects reflect what happens in the world's largest economy. To equate globalization with Americanization is to oversimplify a complex reality.

Nonetheless, several characteristics of the United States make it a center of globalization. America has always been a land of immigration, and its culture and multiethnic society reflect many different parts of the world. America has borrowed freely from a variety of traditions and immigration keeps it open to the rest of the world. This makes the United States a laboratory for cultural experimentation where different traditions are recombined and exported. In addition, because of the size of the American economy, the United States is the largest marketplace in which to test whether a film or song or game will attract large and diverse audiences. Ideas and products flow into the United States freely, and flow out with equal ease—often in commercialized form. Pizza in Asia seems American.[29]

The effects of globalization, however, depend upon the receiver as well as the sender. Already a half century ago, Hannah Arendt wrote that "in reality, the process which Europeans dread as 'Americanization' is the emergence of the modern world with all its perplexities and implications." She speculated that the modernization process that appeared to be American would be accelerated, not halted, by European integration.[30] In Nigeria, where American programs provided more than half the content on television in 1997, "The heavy direct and indirect presence in virtually every key area of Nigerian life assures continued Americanization, not just of television, but of other facets of Nigerian culture."[31] The experience in Japan, however, was very different. "On the surface, the Japanese may appear to be tireless and indiscriminate cultural consumers. But the foreignness of imported culture, and particularly American culture, is filtered through the careful hands of cultural brokers. . . . American culture is deconstructed and re-contextualized into the everyday experience of the people. American popular culture is not the monopoly of Americans: it is a medium through which people around the world constantly reorganize their individual and collective identities."[32]

Many of the mechanisms driving globalization are characteristic features of the U.S. culture and economy. Much of the information revolution originated in the American economy, and a large part of

Figure 2.3 Dimensions of American Attractiveness in the Islamic World

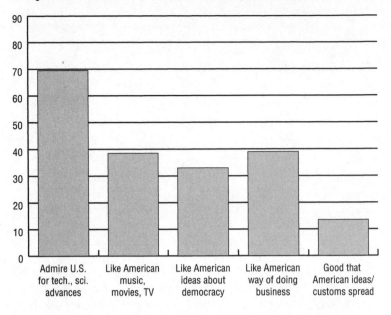

Source: Pew Global Attitudes Project, *What the World Thinks in 2002.*
Median measures in seven countries with majority Muslim populations

the content of global information networks is currently created in the United States. American standards are sometimes hard to avoid, as in Microsoft's Windows or in the rules governing the Internet (though the World Wide Web was invented in Europe). On the other hand, some U.S. standards and practices—from the measurement system of pounds and feet (rather than the metric system) to capital punishment—have encountered puzzlement or even outright hostility. Globalization is more than Americanization, but for those in the antiglobalization movement who want to resist or reshape globalization, anti-Americanism is often a useful weapon and thus its conflation with globalization is to some extent inevitable.

Of particular concern is the role of anti-Americanism in the Islamic world. Compare figure 2.3 with figure 2.1 and you will see that the dimensions of American attraction are different in the Muslim world. A bipartisan panel report issued in October 2003 stated, "Hostility toward America has reached shocking levels. What is required is not merely tactical adaptation, but strategic and radical transformation."[33]

Moreover, the image of the United States has declined there more than elsewhere. In 2003, less than 15 percent of the public in Turkey, Indonesia, Pakistan, and Jordan, and less than 27 percent in Lebanon and Morocco, had a favorable opinion of the United States.[34]

This is a matter of particular concern because some Islamist extremists are willing to use terror to force a return to what they portray as a purer, premodern version of their religion. In some areas, such as the Arab countries, anti-Americanism may be a cover for a more general inability to respond to modernity—witness the slow progress of economic growth and democratization as described in a recent report of the United Nations Development Programme, "Arab Human Development Report 2003."[35] Fouad Ajami, an American academic of Lebanese origin, is correct in saying that America will be resented because our burden is "to come bearing modernism to those who want it but who rail against it at the same time, to represent and embody so much of what the world yearns for and fears." But he is wrong to conclude from this that "Americans need not worry about hearts and minds in foreign lands."[36] The situation he describes has been constant for a number of years, and thus cannot explain the recent downward trajectory of America's reputation in economically successful Muslim countries like Malaysia. The failure of Arab countries to adjust to modernity cannot fully explain the changes in U.S. attractiveness. They are also related to unpopular U.S. policies regarding Iraq and the Israel-Palestine conflict.

The effects of the Iraq War should not be exaggerated. "Dire predictions notwithstanding, Arabs did not rise up to destroy American interests in the Middle East . . . because many of them knew Saddam Hussein's record."[37] As mentioned earlier, images of a country are composed of several elements, and respondents to polls showed a greater dislike of American policies than of American people.[38] Nonetheless, there have been boycotts of American products, and the American share of merchandise exported to the Middle East had already dropped from 18 to 13 percent from the late 1990s to 2001 partly in response to America's "perceived loss of foreign policy legitimacy."[39] Extreme Islamists had already opposed the American campaign against the Taliban in Afghanistan, and Iraq merely increased their opportunities to whip up hatred. But such hatred is increasingly important in a world where small groups can use the Internet to find, recruit, and mobilize like-minded people who previously had greater difficulty in locating each other. As the author Robert Wright has observed, Osama bin Laden's recruiting videos are very effective, "and they'll reach their targeted audience much more efficiently via broadband."[40]

The recent decline in the reported attractiveness of the United States illustrates the point I made in the previous chapter: It is not enough just to have visible power resources. In the case of soft power, the question is what messages are sent and received by whom under which circumstances, and how that affects our ability to obtain the outcomes we want. Messages and images are conveyed partly by government policies at home and abroad, and partly by popular and higher culture. But the same messages are "downloaded" and interpreted with different effects by different receivers in different settings. Soft power is not a constant, but something that varies by time and place.

CULTURE AS A SOURCE OF SOFT POWER

As we know, cultural critics often distinguish between high culture and popular culture. Many observers would agree that American high culture produces significant soft power for the United States. For example, Secretary of State Colin Powell has said, "I can think of no more valuable asset to our country than the friendship of future world leaders who have been educated here."[41] International students usually return home with a greater appreciation of American values and institutions, and, as expressed in a report by an international education group, "The millions of people who have studied in the United States over the years constitute a remarkable reservoir of goodwill for our country."[42] Many of these former students eventually wind up in positions where they can affect policy outcomes that are important to Americans.

The distinguished American diplomat and writer George Kennan is a traditional realist in his concern with balance-of-power politics, but he placed great importance on "cultural contact as a means of combating negative impressions about this country that mark so much of world opinion." Kennan said he would "willingly trade the entire remaining inventory of political propaganda for the results that could be achieved by such means alone." And President Dwight Eisenhower argued for the need "to work out not one method but thousands of methods by which people can gradually learn a little bit more about each other." Indeed, high cultural contacts often produced soft power for the United States during the Cold War. Scores of nongovernmental institutions such as theaters, museums, and opera companies performed in the Soviet Union. One Soviet musician observed that they had been trained to believe in the decadent West, yet year after year great symphony orchestras came from Boston, Philadelphia, New York, Cleveland, and San Francisco. "How could the decadent West produce such great orchestras?"[43]

Academic and scientific exchanges played a significant role in enhancing American soft power. Even while some American skeptics at the time feared that visiting Soviet scientists and KGB agents would "steal us blind," they failed to notice that the visitors vacuumed up political ideas along with scientific secrets. Many such scientists became leading proponents of human rights and liberalization inside the Soviet Union. Starting in the 1950s, the Ford Foundation, the Council of Learned Societies, and the Social Science Research Council worked with eventually 110 American colleges and universities in student and faculty exchanges. Though the Soviet Union demanded a governmental agreement to limit the scope of

such exchanges, some 50,000 Soviets visited the United States between 1958 and 1988 as writers, journalists, officials, musicians,
dancers, athletes, and academics. An even larger number of Americans went to the Soviet Union.

In the 1950s, only 40 to 50 college and graduate students from
each country participated in exchanges, but over time, powerful policy effects can be traced back to even those small numbers. Because
cultural exchanges affect elites, one or two key contacts may have a
major political effect. For example, Aleksandr Yakovlev was strongly
influenced by his studies with the political scientist David Truman at
Columbia University in 1958. Yakovlev eventually went on to become the head of an important institute, a Politburo member, and a
key liberalizing influence on the Soviet leader Mikhail Gorbachev. A
fellow student, Oleg Kalugin, who became a high official in the
KGB, said in looking back from the vantage point of 1997, "Exchanges were a Trojan Horse for the Soviet Union. They played a
tremendous role in the erosion of the Soviet system. . . . They kept
infecting more and more people over the years."[44] The attraction
and soft power that grew out of cultural contacts among elites made
important contributions to American policy objectives.

It is easier to trace specific political effects of high-cultural contacts than to demonstrate the political importance of popular culture. Alexis de Toqueville pointed out in the nineteenth century that
in a democracy there are no restrictions of class or guild on artisans
and their products. Popular taste prevails. In addition, commercial
interests in a capitalist economy seek broad markets that often result
in cultural lowest common denominators. Some believe that American popular culture seduces through sheer force of marketing and
promise of pleasure.[45] Many intellectuals and critics disdain popular
culture because of its crude commercialism. They regard it as providing mass entertainment rather than information and thus having
little political effect. They view popular culture as an anesthetizing
and apolitical opiate for the masses.

Such disdain is misplaced, however, because popular entertainment often contains subliminal images and messages about individu-

alism, consumer choice, and other values that have important political effects. As the author Ben Wattenberg has argued, American culture includes glitz, sex, violence, vapidity and materialism, but that is not the whole story. It also portrays American values that are open, mobile, individualistic, anti-establishment, pluralistic, voluntaristic, populist, and free. "It is that content, whether reflected favorably or unfavorably, that brings people to the box office. That content is more powerful than politics or economics. It drives politics and economics."[46] Or as the poet Carl Sandburg put it in 1961: "What, Hollywood's more important than Harvard? The answer is, not as clean as Harvard, but nevertheless, further reaching."[47]

Even popular sports can play a role in communicating values. "An America is created that is neither military hegemon nor corporate leviathan—a looser place, less rigid and more free, where anyone who works hard shooting a ball or handling a puck can become famous and (yes) rich."[48] And the numbers are large. National Basketball games are broadcast to 750 million households in 212 countries and 42 languages. Major league baseball games flow to 224 countries in 11 languages. The National Football League's Super Bowl attracted an estimated 800 million viewers in 2003. The number of sports viewers rivals the 7.3 billion viewers worldwide who went to see American movies in 2002.

The line between information and entertainment has never been as sharp as some intellectuals imagine, and it is becoming increasingly blurred in a world of mass media. Some lyrics of popular music can have political effects. For example, in the 1990s, the dissident radio station B-92 in Belgrade played over and over the American rap group Public Enemy's lyric "Our freedom of speech is freedom or death—we got to fight the powers that be."[49] Political messages can also be conveyed by the way sports teams or stars conduct themselves, or in the multiple images portrayed by television or cinema. Pictures often convey values more powerfully than words, and Hollywood is the world's greatest promoter and exporter of visual symbols.[50] Even the consumption of fast food can make an implicit statement about rejecting traditional ways. One Indian family described their visit to McDonald's as stepping out for "a slice of America."[51] On the negative side, in the aftermath of the Iraq War a number of Muslims boycotted Coca-Cola and turned to imitations such as Mecca Cola or Muslim Up as "an alternative for all who boycott Zionist products and big American brands."[52]

The political effects of popular culture are not entirely new. The Dutch historian Rob Kroes points out that posters produced for shipping lines and emigration societies in nineteenth-century Europe created an image of the American West as a symbol of freedom long before the twentieth-century consumption revolution. Young Europeans "grew up constructing meaningful worlds that drew upon American ingredients and symbols." American commercial advertisements in 1944 referred to and expanded upon Franklin Roosevelt's four freedoms, thereby reinforcing the official civics lesson. "Generation upon generation of youngsters, growing up in a variety of European settings, West *and* East of the Iron Curtain, have vicariously enjoyed the pleasures of cultural alternatives. . . . Simple items like blue jeans, Coca-Cola, or a cigarette brand acquired an added value that helped these younger generations to give expression to an identity all their own."[53]

This popular-cultural attraction helped the United States to achieve important foreign policy goals. One example was the democratic reconstruction of Europe after World War II. The Marshall Plan and NATO were crucial instruments of economic and military power aimed at achieving that outcome. But popular culture also contributed. For example, the Austrian historian Reinhold Wagnleitner argues that "the fast adaptation of American popular culture by many Europeans after the Second World War certainly contributed positively to the democratization of these societies. It rejuvenated and revitalized European postwar cultures with its elementary connotations of freedom, casualness, vitality, liberality, modernity and youthfulness. . . . Submission to the dictates of the market and business also contained an element of liberation from the straitjackets of traditional customs and mores."[54] The dollars invested by the Marshall Plan were important in achieving American objectives in the reconstruction of Europe, but so also were the ideas transmitted by American popular culture.

Popular cultural attraction also contributed to another major American foreign policy objective—victory in the Cold War. The Soviet Union had impressive military capabilities poised to threaten Western Europe, and in the early postwar period it also possessed important soft-power resources from the appeal of Communist ideology and its record of standing up to Nazi Germany. However, it squandered much of this soft power through its repression at home and in Eastern Europe,[55] and its inept economic performance in its later years (even as its military power increased). Soviet state-run propaganda and culture programs could not keep pace with the influence of America's commercial popular culture in flexibility or attraction. Long before the Berlin Wall fell in 1989, it had been pierced by television and movies. The hammers and bulldozers would not have worked without the years-long transmission of images of the popular culture of the West that breached the Wall before it fell.

Even though the Soviet Union restricted and censored Western films, those that made it through the filters were still capable of having devastating political effects. Sometimes the political effects were direct, although unintended. One Soviet journalist commented after a restricted showing of *On the Beach* and *Dr. Strangelove* (both films were critical of American nuclear weapons policies), "They absolutely shocked us. . . . We began to understand that the same thing would happen to us as to them in a nuclear war." Other unintended political effects were conveyed indirectly. Soviet audiences watching films with apolitical themes nonetheless learned that people in the West did not have to stand in long lines to purchase food, did not live in communal apartments, and owned their own cars. All this invalidated the negative views promulgated by the Soviet media.

Even rock-and-roll music played a part despite Soviet efforts to discourage it. As one of Gorbachev's aides later testified, "The Beatles were our quiet way of rejecting 'the system' while conforming to most of its demands." Georgi Shaknazarov, a high Communist official, summarized the political effects well: "Gorbachev, me, all of us were double-thinkers. We had to balance truth and propaganda in our minds all the time." The corrosive effects on Soviet self-confidence and ideology became clear in their actions when that generation finally came to power in the mid-1980s.[56]

Similarly, Czech Communist officials sentenced a group of young people to prison in the 1950s for playing tapes of "decadent American music," but their efforts turned out to be counterproductive. Milos Forman described how, in the 1960s, "You are listening, you know, to Bill Haley and Elvis Presley and you love it, and then a stern face on the Czech television tells you, 'These apes escaping from the jungle—they are representing the pride of humanity?'. . . Finally you lost total, total, you know, respect." In 1980, after John Lennon was assassinated, a monument to him spontaneously appeared in Prague, and the anniversary of his death was marked by an annual procession for peace and democracy. In 1988, the organizers founded a Lennon Peace Club whose members demanded the removal of Soviet troops.[57] With the passage of time, Lennon trumped Lenin.

As one historian summarized the situation, "However important the military power and political promise of the United States were for setting the foundation for the American successes in Cold War Europe, it was the American economic and cultural attraction that really won over the hearts and minds of the majorities of young people for Western democracy. . . . Whenever real consumption climbed into the ring, chances were high that real socialism had to be counted out."[58] The Cold War was won by a mixture of hard and soft power. Hard power created the stand-off of military containment, but soft power eroded the Soviet system from within. Not all the soft power resources were American—witness the role of the BBC and the Beatles. But it would be a mistake to ignore the role that the attraction of American popular culture played in contributing to the soft part of the equation.

Not only was popular culture relevant to the achievement of American policy goals in Western Europe but it also has been important for a number of other policy goals, including the undercutting of the apartheid regime in South Africa, the increase in the number of democratic governments in Latin America and parts of East Asia, the overthrow of the Milosevic regime in Serbia, pressure for liberalization in Iran, and the consolidation of an open international economic system, to name just a few. Indeed, when South Africa in 1971 was debating whether to allow television into the country, Albert Hertzog, a conservative former minister of Posts and Telegraphs, rejected it as a symbol of Western degeneracy that "would lead to the demoralization of South African civilization and the destruction of apartheid."[59] He turned out to be right.

Similarly, in 1994 Iran's highest-ranking cleric issued a fatwa against satellite television dishes because they would introduce a cheap alien culture and spread the moral diseases of the West.[60] He also turned out to be correct. A decade later, mass demonstrations in Teheran followed the spread of private American TV broadcasts. The stations got their start broadcasting in the Farsi language to the Iranian diaspora in Los Angeles, but they later turned to covering Iran's politics 24 hours a day, and broadcast information to Iran that was not otherwise available there.[61] It was not merely a reactionary minority that was infected by Western ideas. As one professor reported, "In less than a decade after Ayatollah Khomeini's death, these illuminated revolutionaries—the former young veterans of war and revolution—were demanding more freedoms and political rights."[62]

In China, despite censorship, American news seeps across the border to Chinese elites through the Internet, other media, and educational exchanges. In 1989, student protesters in Tiananmen Square constructed a replica of the Statue of Liberty. One dissident told a foreign reporter that when she was forced to listen to local Communist Party leaders rage about America, she would hum Bob Dylan tunes in her head as her own silent revolution. Another reporter observed that "many believe that the recent trickle of Hollywood films into Chinese theatres, along with those illegal DVDs, has played a role in spurring yearnings for accelerated change among ordinary Chinese citizens."[63]

As we learned in chapter 1, popular culture, because it is not under direct control of government, does not always produce the exact policy outcomes that the government might desire. For example, during the Vietnam War, the American government had multiple policy objectives that included both military victory over Communism in Vietnam and political victory over Communism in Central Europe. Popular culture did not help to produce the desired outcomes with regard to the former objective, but it did help to achieve the latter. For example, Reinhold Wagnleitner describes student demonstrations in Austria against the Vietnam War: "We demonstrated in blue jeans and T-shirts and attended sit-ins and teach-ins. What's more, quite a few of us understood what it meant to be able to demonstrate against a war in wartime without being court-martialed. Some of us were also aware that we had learned our peaceful tactics of democratic protest and opposition from the American civil rights movement and the anti-nuclear armament movement. After all, we did not intone the 'Internationale' but instead sang 'We Shall Overcome.'"[64] Protest movements are a part of popular culture that can attract some foreigners to the openness of the United States at the same time that official policies are repelling them.

Popular culture can have contradictory effects on different groups within the same country. It does not provide a uniform soft-power resource. The videos that attract Iranian teenagers offend Iranian mullahs. Thus the repulsion of American popular culture may make it more difficult for the United States to obtain its preferred policy outcomes from the ruling group in the short term, while the attraction of popular culture encourages desired change among younger people in the long term. And sometimes the effects can undercut longer-term American objectives. In Turkey, according to a Turkish journalist, "The spread of American popular culture, primarily among the upper-middle-class and peripherally among the lower-class Turkish population has created in its wake an opposition to the ideology behind it. The resurgence of fundamentalism in recent years which poses a serious threat to secularism, is responsible for creating the rift that has opened up between the

Americanized privileged class, the lower middle class, and poor."[65] Yet even in the tense period after 9/11, and despite visa restrictions, a survey conducted by the British Council among 5,000 students in nine Muslim countries showed that the United States was still the first choice for youngsters in Egypt, Turkey, and Saudi Arabia as a location for pursuing education abroad.[66] Ambivalence is a common reaction to the United States, and where there is ambivalence there is scope for policy to try to improve the ratio of the positive to the negative dimensions.

Finally, the instruments of popular culture are not static. Whether the influence of American culture will increase or decrease in the future is uncertain. In part the outcome will depend on whether unpopular policies eventually spill over and make general reactions to American culture more negative. It will also depend on independent market changes that have nothing to do with politics. For example, American films continue to rake in nearly 80 percent of the film industry's worldwide revenues, but American TV has seen a decline in its international market share in recent years. Television appeals to a more segmented market and local content has proved to be more important in reaching national audiences than the peek into U.S. culture provided by the typical American product.[67] Nielson Media Research has found that 71 percent of the top ten programs in 60 surveyed countries were locally produced, representing a steady increase over the preceding years. The causes seem related more to market changes and economies of scale in satisfying local tastes than to political reactions.[68]

Moreover, the absorption of American popular culture by foreign audiences may make it appear less exotic over time, and thus less fascinating to them. Something similar happened with the European reception of American Wild West shows in the nineteenth century, and already American MTV has lost ground to local imitators. One expert speculates that "globalization of American popular culture, as we know and debate it today, may well prove to be a temporary phenomenon, an issue internationally only so long as it takes to generate a local response that tests which premises can be successfully adapted to local circumstances and expectations."[69] Whether the loss of exoticism will be serious in terms of soft-power resources or not is difficult to predict.

In television news, however, there has been a clear political change. During the Gulf War, CNN and BBC had the field largely to themselves as they framed the issues. For example, Iraq's invasion of Kuwait in August 1991 was described in terms of Iraqi aggression rather than recovering the lost province of Kuwait, which is how the Iraqis saw it. (India framed its invasion of its ancient province of Goa the same way, and there was little significant international reaction.) By the time of the Iraq War, Al Jazeera and others were active competitors in framing the issues. For instance, the same image of moving forces could accurately be described by CNN as "coalition forces advance" or by Al Jazeera as "invading forces advance." The net effect was a reduction in American soft power in the region when 2003 is compared with 1991.

Now France has decided to create its own multilingual television news channel. It concluded that "Al Jazeera is proof that this monopoly can be broken and that there is a real demand for news that is not Anglo-American."[70] Some analysts believe that "the American dominance in the global communication flow is less powerful than it was in the past. On the contrary, a growing concern is not the old complaint of excessive American cultural influence around the world, but the astonishing speed with which the United States is selling off its popular culture industries to foreign buyers."[71]

It is worth noting that while American companies still dominate in terms of global brands, market changes have produced an increased fragmentation of brands. A decade ago it was assumed that as barriers to trade came down, brands with global scale would drive out local brands. In fact, as concerns about local autonomy have intersected with technologies that allow economies of scale to be achieved in production of discrete specialized products, the standardization of brands has come under challenge. Coca-Cola owns more than 200 brands (often not openly linked to the parent company), McDonald's varies its menus by regions, and MTV has responded with different programs for different countries.[72] Even before the political boycotts that followed the Iraq War, market trends were reducing the dominance of American brands. The popular cultural resources that can produce American soft power are important, but they are far from static.

DOMESTIC VALUES AND POLICIES

The United States, like other countries, expresses its values in what it does as well as what it says. Political values like democracy and human rights can be powerful sources of attraction, but it is not enough just to proclaim them. During the Cold War, President Eisenhower worried that the practice of racial segregation in the American South was alienating the newly independent countries in Africa. Others watch how Americans implement our values at home as well as abroad. A Swedish diplomat recently told me, "All countries want to promote the values we believe in. I think the most criticized part of the U.S.'s (and possibly most rich countries') soft-power 'packaging' is the perceived double standard and inconsistencies."[73] Perceived hypocrisy is particularly corrosive of power that is based on proclaimed values. Those who scorn or despise us for hypocrisy are less likely to want to help us achieve our policy objectives.

Even when honestly applied, American values can repel some people at the same time that they attract others. Individualism and liberties are attractive to many people, but repulsive to some, particularly fundamentalists. For example, American feminism, open sexuality, and individual choices are profoundly subversive in patriarchal societies. One of the terrorist pilots who spent time in the United States before the attack on September 11 is reported to have said he did not like the United States because it is "too lax. I can go anywhere I want and they can't stop me."[74] Some religious fundamentalists hate the United States precisely because of our values of openness, tolerance, and opportunity. More typical, however, is the reaction of a Chinese writer who disagreed with his government's criticism of the United States in 2003: "Amid this fog of nationalist emotion, it is all the more remarkable that so many Chinese have managed to keep their faith in American-style democracy. They yearn for a deeper change in their own country's political system."[75]

Admiration for American values does not mean that others want to imitate all the ways by which Americans implement them. Despite admiration for the American practice of freedom of speech, countries like Germany and South Africa have histories that make them wish to prohibit hate crimes that could not be punished under the American First Amendment. And while many Europeans admire America's devotion to freedom, they prefer policies at home that temper neoliberal economic principles and individualism with a greater concern for society and community. In 1991, two out of three Czechs, Poles, Hungarians, and Bulgarians thought the United States was a good influence on their respective countries, but fewer than one in four in each country wanted to import the American economic model.[76] If anything, the Iraq War sharpened the perceived contrast in values between the United States and Europe. A poll conducted by the German Marshall Fund in June 2003 found agreement on both sides of the Atlantic that Europeans and Americans have different social and cultural values.[77]

As Figure 2.1 showed, half of the populations of the countries polled in 2002 liked American ideas about democracy, but only a third thought it good if American ideas and customs spread in their country. Although two-thirds of Africans liked American ideas about democracy, only one-third of the populations of Muslim countries like them.[78] This is not entirely new. In the 1980s, public opinion in four major European countries rated the United States as performing well in economic opportunities, rule of law, religious freedom, and artistic diversity. But fewer than half of British, German, and Spanish respondents felt the United States was a desirable model for other countries.[79] How America behaves at home can enhance its image and perceived legitimacy, and that in turn can help advance its foreign policy objectives. It does not mean that others need or want to become American clones.

American performance on implementing our political values at home is mixed. As noted earlier, the United States ranks at or near the top in health expenditure, higher education, books published, computer and Internet usage, acceptance of immigrants, and employment. But America is not at the top in life expectancy, primary education, job security, access to health care, or income equality. And high rankings in areas like the incidence of homicide and the percentage of the population in jail reduce attractiveness. On the other hand, there is little evidence for the cultural decline that some pessimists proclaim, and many American domestic problems are shared by other postmodern societies.

Crime, divorce rates, and teenage pregnancy are worse today than in the 1950s, but all three measures improved considerably in the 1990s, and, writes a former president of Harvard University, "There is no reliable evidence that American students are learning less in school, or that the American Dream is vanishing, or that the environment is more polluted."[80] Health, environment, and safety conditions have improved.[81] Most children still live with both natural parents, and the divorce rate has stabilized.

Trust in government has declined over recent decades, and that has led some observers to worry about American democracy. But the polling evidence is not matched in all behaviors. For example, the Internal Revenue Service reports no increase in cheating on taxes.[82] By many accounts, government officials and legislators have become less corrupt than they were a few decades ago.[83] Voluntary mail return of census forms increased to 67 percent in 2000, reversing a 30-year decline in return rates since 1970.[84] Voting rates have declined from 62 percent to 50 percent over the past 40 years, but the decline stopped in 2000, and the current rate is not as low as it was in the 1920s. Moreover, polls show that nonvoters are no more alienated or mistrustful of government than voters are.[85]

Despite predictions of institutional crisis expressed in the aftermath of the tightly contested 2000 presidential election, constitutional procedures were widely accepted and the incoming Bush administration was able to govern effectively. Nor does the decline of trust in government seem to have greatly diminished American soft power, if only because most other developed countries seem to be experiencing a similar phenomenon. Canada, Britain, France, Sweden, and Japan have experienced a loss of confidence in institutions that seems to be rooted in the greater individualism and diminished deference to authority that are characteristic of postmodern societies.[86]

Similarly, while there have been changes in participation in voluntary organizations, changes in social participation do not seem to have eroded American soft power. For one thing, the absolute levels of engagement remain remarkably high on many indicators. Three-quarters of Americans feel connected to their communities, and say the quality of life here is excellent or good. According to a 2001 poll, over 100 million Americans volunteered their time to help solve problems in their communities, and 60 million volunteer on a regular basis.[87] Americans remain more likely than citizens of most other countries, with the exception of a few small nations of Northern Europe, to be involved in voluntary organizations.[88]

Even after 9/11, America remains a country of immigration. People want to come to America, and they often do well here. By 1998, Chinese and Indian engineers were running one-quarter of Silicon Valley's high-technology businesses,[89] and such upward mobility makes America a magnet. Foreigners can envisage themselves as Americans, and many successful Americans "look like" them. Moreover, connections of individuals in the diasporas such as the Indian and Chinese with their countries of origin help to convey accurate and positive information about the United States.

Certainly a decline in the quality of American society or unattractive policies at home could reduce our attractiveness and that could damage our soft power. But when other countries share similar problems, comparisons are less invidious and less damaging to our soft power. As a Population Council report pointed out, "Trends like unwed motherhood, rising divorce rates, smaller household and the feminization of poverty are not unique to America, but are occurring worldwide."[90] Similarly, respect for authority and institutions has declined since 1960 throughout the Western world, and American levels are not much different than those of other advanced Western societies. In fact, American levels of charitable giving and community service are generally higher.[91] Problems that are shared with other societies are less likely to cut into our soft-power resources.

American soft power is eroded more by policies like capital punishment or the absence of gun control, where we are the deviants in opinion among advanced countries. American support for the death penalty, for example, meets disapproval from two-thirds of the public in Great Britain, France, Germany, and Italy.[92] Similarly, the American domestic response to terrorism after 9/11 runs some risk of reducing our soft-power resources. Attitudes toward immigration have hardened, and new visa procedures have discouraged some foreign students. A decline in religious tolerance toward Muslims hurts the image of the United States in Muslim countries such as Pakistan and Indonesia as well as in the Arab world.

Although President Bush wisely included Muslim clerics in the mourning ceremony at the National Cathedral and invited them to the White House after 9/11, the Pentagon chose Franklin Graham, a Christian evangelist who branded Islam a "very wicked and evil religion," to conduct its Good Friday service in 2003.[93] Some Americans have cast Islam in the role that was once played by Communism and the Soviet Union. The past president of the Southern Baptist Convention described Muhammad as "a demon-possessed pedophile." Such fringe views are often magnified abroad, particularly when they appear to have official sanction. The result, in the experience of Dr. Clive Calver of World Relief, is that such comments are "used to indict all Americans and used to indict all Christians. It obviously puts lives and livelihoods of people overseas at risk."[94] Religion is a double-edged sword as an American soft-power resource, and how it cuts depends on who is wielding it.

Also damaging to American attractiveness is the perception that the United States has not lived up to its own profession of values in its response to terrorism. It is perhaps predictable when Amnesty

International referred to the Guantanamo Bay detentions as a "human rights scandal," and Human Rights Watch charged the United States with hypocrisy that undercuts its own policies and puts itself in "a weak position to insist on compliance from others."[95] Even more damaging perhaps is when such criticism came from conservative pro-American sources. The *Financial Times* worried that "the very character of American democracy has been altered. Most countries have chosen to adjust the balance between liberty and security since September 11. But in America, the adjustment has gone beyond mere tinkering to the point where fundamental values may be jeopardised." Meanwhile *The Economist* argued that President Bush "is setting up a shadow court system outside the reach of either Congress or America's judiciary, and answerable only to himself. . . . Mr. Bush rightly noted that American ideals have been a beacon of hope to others around the world. In compromising those ideals in this matter, Mr. Bush is not only dismaying America's friends, but also blunting one of America's most powerful weapons against terrorism."[96] Pictures of prisoner abuse at Iraq's Abu Ghraib prison achieved iconic status after being published around the world. It remains to be seen how lasting such damage will be to America's ability to obtain the outcomes it wants from other countries. At a minimum, it tends to make our preaching on human rights policies appear hypocritical to some people.

FOREIGN POLICY
SUBSTANCE AND STYLE

The attractiveness of the United States also depends very much upon the values we express through the substance and style of our foreign policy. All countries pursue their national interest in foreign policy, but there are choices to be made about how broadly or narrowly we define our national interest, as well as the means by which we pursue it. After all, soft power is about mobilizing cooperation from others without threats or payments. Since it depends on the currency of attraction rather than force or payoffs, soft power depends in part on how we frame our own objectives. Policies based on broadly inclusive and far-sighted definitions of the national interest are easier to make attractive to others than policies that take a narrow and myopic perspective.

Similarly, policies that express important values are more likely to be attractive when the values are shared. The Norwegian author Geir Lundestad has referred to America's success in Europe in the latter half of the twentieth century as an empire by invitation. "On the value side, federalism, democracy and open markets represented core American values. This is what America exported."[97] And because of far-sighted policies like the Marshall Plan, Europeans were happy to accept. But the resulting soft power depended in part on the considerable overlap of culture and values between the United States and Europe.

In the twenty-first century the United States has an interest in maintaining a degree of international order. It needs to influence distant governments and organizations on a variety of issues such as proliferation of weapons of mass destruction, terrorism, drugs, trade, resources, and ecological damage that affect Americans as well as others. The United States, like nineteenth-century Britain, also has an interest in keeping international markets and global commons, such as the oceans, open to all. To a large extent, international order is a public good—something everyone can consume without diminishing its availability to others.[98] Of course, pure public goods are rare. And sometimes things that look good to Americans may not look good to everyone else, and that is why consultation is important.

A large country like the United States gains doubly when it promotes public goods: from the goods themselves, and from the way that being a major provider legitimizes and increases its soft power. Thus when the Bush administration announced that it would increase its development assistance and take the lead in combating HIV/AIDS, it meant the United States would not only benefit from the markets and stability that might be produced, but also by enhancing its attractiveness or soft-power resources. International development is also an important global public good. Nonetheless, American foreign aid was .1 percent of GDP, roughly one-third of the European levels, and protectionist trade measures, particularly in agriculture and textiles, hurt poor countries more than the value of the aid provided. According to one index that tries to evaluate how well rich countries help the poor by including trade, environment, investment, migration, and peacekeeping along with actual aid, the United States ranks twentieth out of 21 (just ahead of Japan).[99] Despite the Bush administration's efforts, the United States has a distance to go to gain soft-power resources in the development area.

Foreign policies also produce soft power when they promote broadly shared values such as democracy and human rights. Americans have wrestled with how to integrate our values with other interests since the early days of the republic, and the main views cut across party lines. Realists like John Quincy Adams warned that the United States "goes not abroad in search of monsters to destroy," and we should not involve ourselves "beyond the power of extrication in all the wars of interest and intrigue."[100] Others follow the tradition of Woodrow Wilson and emphasize democracy and human rights as foreign policy objectives. As we shall see in chapter 5, today's neoconservatives are, in effect, right-wing Wilsonians, and they are interested in the soft power that can be generated by the promotion of democracy.

During the 2000 election campaign, when George W. Bush frequently expressed traditional realist warnings that the United States should not become overextended, leading neoconservatives urged him to make human rights, religious freedom, and democracy priorities for American foreign policy and "not to adopt a narrow view of U.S. national interests."[101] After 9/11, Bush's policy changed and he spoke of the need to use American power to bring democracy to the Middle East. As Lawrence Kaplan and William Kristol put it, "When it comes to dealing with tyrannical regimes like Iraq, Iran and, yes, North Korea, the U.S. should seek transformation, not coexistence, as a primary aim of U.S. foreign policy. As such, it commits the U.S. to the task of maintaining and enforcing a decent world order."[102]

The neoconservatives are correct that such a world order could be a global public good, but they are mistaken to assume that their vision will be shared by all those affected by it. Whether the neoconservative approach creates rather than consumes American soft power depends not only on the results but also on who is consulted and who decides. The neoconservatives pay less heed than traditional Wilsonians to consultation through international institutions. But because the currency of soft power is attraction, it is often easier to generate and wield in a multilateral context.

In recent years, other countries have increasingly complained about the unilateralism of American foreign policy. Of course such differences are a matter of degree, and there are few countries that are pure unilateralists or multilateralists. International concerns about unilateralism began well before George W. Bush became president, and involved Congress as well as the executive branch. The president has disclaimed the label but most observers describe his administration as divided between traditional pragmatists and a more ideological school that the columnist Charles Krauthammer celebrated as "the new unilateralism."[103]

The "new unilateralists" advocate an assertive approach to promoting American values. They worry about a flagging of internal will and a reluctance to turn a unipolar moment into a unipolar era.[104] American intentions are good, American hegemony is benevolent, and that should end the discussion. To them, multilateralism means "submerging American will in a mush of collective decision-making—you have sentenced yourself to reacting to events or passing the buck to multilingual committees with fancy acronyms."[105] They deny that American "arrogance" is a problem. Rather, the problem is "the inescapable reality of American power in its many forms."[106] Policy is legitimized by its origins in a democracy and by the outcome—whether it results in an advance of freedom and democracy. That post hoc legitimization will more than compensate for any loss of legitimacy through unilateralism.

Unfortunately, the approach of the new unilateralists is not very convincing to other countries whose citizens observe that Americans are not immune from hubris and self-interest. Americans do not always have all the answers. As one realist put it, "If we were truly acting in the interests of others as well as our own, we would presumably accord to others a substantive role and, by doing so, end up embracing some form of multilateralism. Others, after all, must be supposed to know their interests better than we can know them."[107] Since the currency of soft power is attraction based on shared values and the justness and duty of others to contribute to policies consistent with those shared values, multilateral consultations are more likely to generate soft power than mere unilateral assertion of the values.

There is increasing evidence that the policies and tone of the new unilateralists were directly responsible for the decline of America's attractiveness abroad. A survey conducted a month before September 11, 2001, found that Western Europeans already described the Bush administration's approach to foreign policy as unilateralist. Nearly two years later, the Iraq War hardened these perceptions: pluralities of respondents said that American foreign policy had a negative effect on their views of the United States.[108] In a dramatic turnabout from the Cold War, strong majorities in Europe now see U.S. unilateralism as an important international threat to Europe in the next ten years. Nearly nine in ten French and Germans share this point of view, perceiving the threat of U.S. unilateralism as comparable to the threats represented by North Korea's or Iran's developing weapons of mass destruction. Even among the Iraq coalition allies, Britain and Poland, two-thirds of these countries' populations agree that U.S. unilateralism is an important threat.[109]

The struggle between multilateralists and unilateralists in the Congress created a schizophrenic American foreign policy even before the current administration. The United States negotiated multilateral projects such as the Law of the Seas Treaty, the Comprehensive Test Ban Treaty, the Land Mines Treaty, the International Criminal Court, and the Kyoto Protocol on climate change, but Congress failed to ratify them. In some cases, such as the Kyoto Protocol, President Bush simply pronounced it "dead" without offering any alternatives. Whatever the flaws of the Kyoto Protocol, the way Bush's policy toward it was handled resulted in foreign reactions that undermined American soft power. And in the run-up to the Iraq War, many other countries felt that although the pragmatists prevailed in seeking Security Council resolution 1441 aimed at removing Iraq's weapons of mass destruction in the fall of 2002, the unilateralists had already decided on going to war. The result was a stalemated diplomacy that turned into a dispute about American power.

Ever since Athens transformed the Delian League into an empire in the fifth century B.C., smaller allies have been torn between anxieties over abandonment or entrapment. The fact that American allies have been able to voice their concerns helps to explain why American alliances persisted so long after Cold War threats receded. Membership in a web of multilateral institutions ranging from the UN to NATO has been called a constitutional bargain.[110] Seen in the light of a constitutional bargain, the multilateralism of American preeminence was a key to its longevity, because it reduced the incentives for constructing countervailing alliances.

But giving others a voice also tempered American objectives and made them more acceptable to others. Former Secretary of Defense Robert McNamara, one of the architects of the Vietnam War, subsequently concluded, "If we can't persuade nations with comparable values of the merit of our cause, we'd better re-examine our reasoning. If we'd followed that rule in Vietnam, we wouldn't have been there. None of our allies supported us."[111] Multilateralism helps to legitimate American power, but paying attention to allies also shapes our policies, and the new unilateralists felt that those costs outweighed the soft-power benefits. Vice President Dick Cheney warned, "Strength, and resolve and decisive action defeat attacks before they can arrive on our shore." It is dangerous to rely too heavily on reaching international consensus, asserted Cheney, because that approach "amounts to a policy of doing exactly nothing."[112]

By and large, the American public has supported U.S. involvement in multilateral institutions and appreciated the legitimacy that participation has conferred on U.S. foreign policy. As we will see in chapter 3, support for the United Nations has had its ups and downs over the past 50 years, but in the aftermath of the Iraq War, two-thirds of Americans still voiced favorable opinions of the United Nations.[113] Before the war, polls consistently showed that public support for military action was strongest if the U.S. acted with the backing of the Security Council. There is further evidence that unilateralism makes a majority of Americans uncomfortable: after the war, two-thirds (67 percent) said that the tendency to go it alone was an important threat to the United States over the next ten years.[114]

Of course, not all multilateral arrangements are good, and a general presumption in favor of multilateralism need not be a straitjacket. When the United States occasionally goes it alone in pursuit of public goods, the nature of the broadly shared value of the ends can sometimes compensate for the means in legitimizing the action and preserving soft power. But the new unilateralists' efforts in recent years to elevate unilateralism from an occasional tactic to a full-fledged strategy has been costly to American soft power. That loss of soft power can be costly for hard power. For example, in July 2003, when the United States encountered more resistance in Iraq than it had planned for, it had half the Army's 33 active-duty combat brigades tied down there. It sought peacekeeping and policing forces from India, Pakistan, France, and other countries, but India, France, Germany, and others responded that they would send forces only under UN auspices.[115]

Regardless of what tactics are used, style also matters, and humility is an important aspect of foreign-policy style. During the 2000 political campaign, George W. Bush described American power well: "Our nation stands alone right now in the world in terms of power. And that's why we've got to be humble and yet project strength in a way that promotes freedom. . . . If we are an arrogant nation, they'll view us that way, but if we're a humble nation, they'll respect us."[116] His statement was perceptive, yet polls show that foreign nations consider his administration arrogant. Within a few months of Bush's address, for the first time America's European allies joined other countries in refusing to reelect the United States to the UN Human Rights Commission. One observer noted that at the start of his administration, President Bush "contrived to prove his own theory that arrogance provokes resentment for a country that, long before his arrival, was already the world's most conspicuous and convenient target."[117]

A sampling of public opinion in 11 countries by the BBC in 2003 found that many people saw the United States as an arrogant superpower that poses a greater danger to world peace than North Korea does. Sixty-five percent overall—and a majority in every country, *including* the United States—said that America was arrogant.[118] Writing in Britain's *Financial Times*, Philip Stephens stated, "This shift in world opinion has much to do with rhetoric and tone of voice. Time after time the quiet diplomacy of Colin Powell's State Department and the cautious deliberations of George W. Bush himself have been undercut by the bellicose statements of Mr. Rumsfeld and of Dick Cheney, the Vice President. The loud-hailer rhetoric often turns out to be at odds with the pragmatic policy choices."[119]

After the Iraq War, Irwin Stelzer, an American conservative living in London, reported "an erosion of support for the US from British friends who cannot by any stretch of the imagination be considered anti-American. The swagger of the US Defence Department inclines them to give credence to charges that unconstrained American power exists, and is likely to be deployed in a manner that threatens the security of America's allies."[120] One reporter observed about a meeting with Europeans that Undersecretary of State John Bolton seemed to enjoy unnecessarily insulting other countries.[121] Yet former President George H. W. Bush had advised after the Iraq War, "You've got to reach out to the other person. You've got to convince them that long-term friendship should trump short-term adversity." Brent Scowcroft, his national security adviser, warned that "ad hoc coalitions of the willing can give us the image of arrogance, and if you get to the point where everyone hopes that the US gets a black eye because we're so obnoxious, then we'll be totally hamstrung."[122] A century ago Teddy Roosevelt noted, when you have a big stick, it is wise to speak softly. Otherwise you undercut your soft power. In short, though it is true that America's size creates a necessity to lead and makes it a target for resentment as well as admiration, both the substance and style of our foreign policy can make a difference to our image of legitimacy, and thus to our soft power.

T HE IMAGE OF THE UNITED STATES and its attractiveness to others is a composite of many different ideas and attitudes. It depends in part on culture, in part on domestic policies and values, and in part on the substance, tactics, and style of our foreign policies. Over the years, these three resources have often produced soft power—the ability to get the outcomes America wanted by attracting rather than coercing others. All three are important, but policy substance and style are both the most volatile and the most susceptible to government control. In any event, we have seen that soft power is not static. Resources change with the changing context. They have varied in the past and will continue to do so in the future. Historical trends from the Cold War era may not prove reliable guides when forecasting the ebb and flow of American soft power in the war on terrorism. In chapter 4 we will discuss the extent to which policies of public diplomacy can enhance that soft power. But first, we should look at the soft power of others besides the United States.

APPENDIX

Figure 2.4   Dimensions of American Attractiveness in Europe

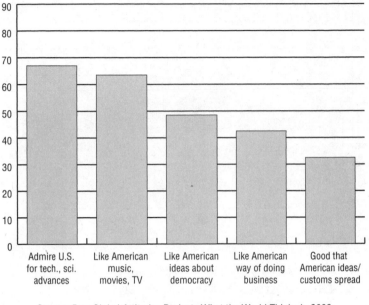

Source: Pew Global Attitudes Project, *What the World Thinks in 2002.*
Median measures in ten European countries

Figure 2.5   Dimensions of American Attractiveness in Southeast Asia

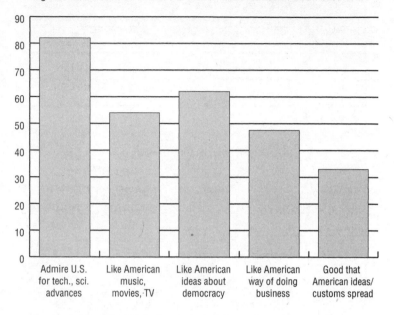

Source: Pew Global Attitudes Project, *What the World Thinks in 2002.*
Median measures in six Asian countries (non-Muslim majority populations)

Figure 2.6   Dimensions of American Attractiveness in Africa

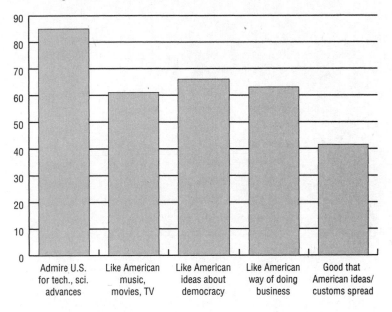

Source: Pew Global Attitudes Project, *What the World Thinks in 2002.*
Median measures in ten African countries

Figure 2.7   Dimensions of U.S. Attractiveness in the Americas

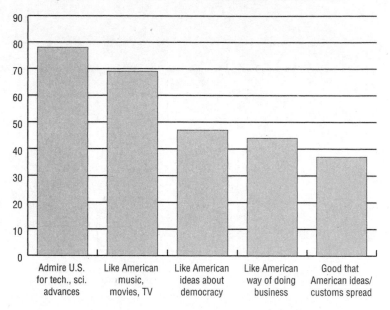

Source: Pew Global Attitudes Project, *What the World Thinks in 2002.*
Median measures in nine North and South American countries (excluding the U.S.)

CHAPTER THREE

Others' Soft Power

THE UNITED STATES has enormous soft-power resources, and has often used them effectively to achieve outcomes it wanted. Given America's role as a leader of the information age, the opportunities for American soft power should increase if the nation acts skillfully. But the United States is not alone. Others, both countries and nonstate actors, also possess soft power that can be used to help or hinder the United States' achievement of its preferred outcomes.

THE SOVIET UNION

During the Cold War, America's primary competitor in soft-power resources was the Soviet Union, which engaged in a broad campaign to convince the rest of the world of the attractiveness of its Communist system. As mentioned in chapter 1, after 1945 the Soviet Union attracted many in Europe because of its resistance to Hitler, and in colonized areas such as Africa and Asia because of its opposition to European imperialism. The utopian promise of Communism appealed to many people in various parts of the world, and Moscow used local Communist Parties to serve its interests. The Soviet Union also spent billions on an active public diplomacy program that included promoting its high culture, broadcasting, disseminating disinformation about the West, and sponsoring antinuclear protests, peace movements, and youth organizations.

High economic growth rates in the early period of postwar reconstruction bolstered Soviet claims that it would overtake the West. When Nikita Khrushchev visited the United States in 1959, many people took seriously his claim that the Soviet Union would one day bury the United States. The apparent success of the Soviet planned economy provided the Soviets not only with hard resources but also a degree of soft-power resources as well. The 1957 launch of *Sputnik*, the first space satellite, led many people in European countries to believe that the USSR was ahead of the United States in space, and that science occupied a more respected position in Soviet culture than in American.[1] These investments not only had military implications but also advanced Soviet soft power and the Soviet Union's claims that Communism was "scientific socialism."

The USSR also placed great emphasis on demonstrating the superiority of its cultural and educational systems, spending large sums on the arts. The Bolshoi and Kirov ballet companies and Soviet symphony orchestras attracted wide acclaim (though socialist realist art did not.) The Soviets also invested heavily in sports, and over the decades Soviet Olympic teams won more gold medals than the U.S. in the Winter Games, and were second in the Summer Games. Popular culture, however, was an entirely different story. The closed nature of the Soviet system and its constant efforts to exclude bourgeois cultural influences meant that the Soviet Union ceded the battle for mass culture, never competing with American global influence in film, television, or popular music. As we saw in the last chapter, American music and films leaked into the Soviet Union with profound effects, but the indigenous Soviet products never found an overseas market. There was no socialist Elvis. Government-sponsored efforts like the magazine *Soviet Life* or the television series *Russian Language and People* were faint echoes in the empty hall of popular culture. Soviet culture did not generate many soft-power resources.

Polls in Western Europe show how ineffective the Soviets were at expanding their soft power. Their efforts did little to increase their attractiveness. In 1959, for example, 32 percent of Italians, 24 percent of British, 17 percent of French, and only 7 percent of Germans had a good opinion of the USSR. Ratings for the United States were much higher. In 1981, 21 percent of Italians, 12 percent of British, 19 percent of French and 8 percent of Germans had a favorable view of the Soviets. Only in 1989, after Mikhail Gorbachev finally changed Soviet policies and brought an end to the Cold War, did Soviet favorability ratings rise to 65 percent among Italians, 59 percent among British, 45 percent among French, and a remarkable 71 percent among Germans (albeit the Soviet ratings were still lower than those for the United States).[2] Gorbachev's policy of *glasnost* (openness) had a positive effect on Soviet soft power.

In science and technology, classical music, ballet, and athletics, Soviet culture was attractive, but the absence of popular cultural exports limited its impact. Even more important, Soviet propaganda was inconsistent with its policies. At home, Soviet claims were undercut by the revelations that followed de-Stalinization in 1956, and later by an economic slowdown as the central planning system failed to keep pace with markets that were becoming ever more flexible in the advancing information age. In foreign policy, Soviet claims to leadership of progressive anti-imperial forces were belied by the invasion of Hungary in 1956 and Czechoslovakia in 1968 and the crackdown in Poland in 1981. A closed system, lack of an attractive popular culture, and heavy-handed foreign policies meant that the Soviet Union was never a serious competitor with the United States in soft power during the Cold War.

EUROPE

Currently, the closest competitor to the United States in soft power resources is Europe. European art, literature, music, design, fashion, and food have long served as global cultural magnets. Taken individually, many European states have a strong cultural attractiveness: half of the ten most widely spoken languages in the world are European.[3] Spanish and Portuguese link Iberia to Latin America, English is the language of the United States and the far-flung Commonwealth, and there are nearly 50 Francophone countries who meet at a biannual summit at which they discuss policies and celebrate their status as countries having French in common. France spends close to $1 billion a year to spread French civilization around the world. As seen from distant Singapore, "France's soft power has been clearly maintained or even increased in the past fifty years, although Paris may no longer be the prime intellectual, cultural and philosophical capital of the world."[4] But the soft power does not rest only on language use. One advocate of "Asian values," former Prime Minister Mahathir of Malaysia, refers to the new concerns about environment and human rights as "European values."[5]

In terms of other potential soft power resources:

* France ranks first in Nobel Prizes for literature; Britain, Germany, and Spain are third, fourth and fifth.
* Britain, Germany, and France rank second, third, and fourth in Nobel Prizes in physics and chemistry.
* Britain, Germany, and France are third, fourth, and fifth (behind the U.S. and Japan) in music sales.
* Germany and Britain are third and fourth in book sales, and fourth and fifth as Internet website hosts.
* France ranks ahead of the United States in attracting tourists (albeit heavily from its neighbors in Europe).
* Britain is first and Germany is second in attracting applications for political asylum.
* France, Germany, Italy, and Britain have higher life expectancy at birth than does the U.S.
* Almost all European countries outrank the United States in overseas development assistance as a percent of GDP.[6]
* Soccer, Europe's primary sport, is far more popular globally than American football or baseball.
* European popular music has a global following.
* European multinationals have brands with global name recognition.

✳ Though much smaller than the United States, Britain and
France each spend about the same as the United States on
public diplomacy.

No single European state can hope to compete with the United
States in size, but taken as a whole, Europe has a market of equiva-
lent size, and a somewhat larger population. Furthermore, the European Union as a symbol of a uniting Europe itself carries a good deal
of soft power. Polls conducted in July 2002 found that a majority of
Americans had a favorable image of the European Union, and
ranked it fourth for its influence in the world behind the United
States, Britain, and China.[7] The idea that war is now unthinkable
among countries that fought bitterly for centuries, and that Europe
has become an island of peace and prosperity creates a positive image in much of the world. In the late 1980s, when Eastern Europeans were asked which countries would serve as models for their
future in terms of economic growth, equality, democracy, and individual freedoms, Western Europe outranked the United States.
Even in pro-American Poland, a survey of Warsaw youth in 1986
showed that half would choose a West European country as a place
to live if given a free choice, compared to 8 percent who would
choose the United States and 4 percent who would opt for another
socialist country. Both the Polish and Czechoslovak election campaigns in 1989 were marked by the slogan "back to Europe."[8]
    With the end of the Cold War, the goal of joining the European
Union became a magnet that meant the entire region of Eastern Europe oriented itself toward Brussels. In a 1991 poll, 75 percent in
Czechoslovakia had a favorable view of the European Economic
Community (64 percent said the United States was a good influence).[9] The newly free countries adapted their domestic laws and
policies to conform with West European standards. Ironically, in
2003, a higher portion of people in the 13 candidate countries
ranked the EU as attractive (54 percent) than did citizens of the 15
EU countries themselves (47 percent).[10] The historian Timothy
Garton Ash has written that Europe's "soft power is demonstrated

by the fact that not only millions of individuals but also whole states want to enter it. Turkey, for example."[11] In Turkey, the desire to join the EU led the government to pass difficult legislation reducing the role of the military in politics and improving Turkey's record on human rights issues.

This is why Secretary of Defense Donald Rumsfeld's efforts during the Iraq War to divide "old and new Europe" were so clumsy and heavy-handed. While the United States still enjoys a fund of goodwill in Eastern Europe left over from its opposition to the Soviet Union during the Cold War, polls show that Eastern Europeans see their long-run future tied to the European Union and do not wish to have to choose between Europe and the United States. The EU knows that it holds this soft-power card and has used it to obtain the policy outcomes it preferred. For example, when President Bush called European leaders in December 2002 to urge them to admit Turkey to the European Union, they regarded his calls as a cynical ploy to persuade Turkey to support the United States over Iraq, and he was told that this would be a purely European decision.[12]

A measure of the EU's emerging soft power is the view that it is a positive force for solving global problems. In the wake of the Iraq War, Eastern Europeans and Turks gave the EU higher marks than the United States for playing a positive role on a variety of issues ranging from fighting terrorism to reducing poverty to protecting the environment. Despite the fact that many Eastern European leaders supported the U.S.-led war, their citizens felt that the EU plays a more positive role than the U.S. on a variety of transnational issues.[13] Shirley Williams, a British political leader, has concluded, "Europe's military strength, its 'hard power,' may be derisory as Donald Rumsfeld implied. Its 'soft power' . . . is formidable indeed."[14] The vast majority of Americans recognize this as well: nearly nine in ten agree that the EU can help solve world problems through diplomacy, trade, and development aid even though it is not as militarily powerful as the U.S.[15]

Of course, Europe still faces a number of problems as its division over Iraq illustrated. It is united on trade, monetary policy, and agriculture, and increasingly on human rights and criminal laws. It is seeking a stronger constitution, which will create a presidency and a foreign minister, but when there is disagreement, foreign and defense policies will remain effectively with national governments. Money and guns, the traditional high cards of hard state power, remain primarily under the control of the member states. Moreover, bureaucratic obstacles and rigid labor markets may hamper rapid economic growth, and underlying demographic trends are unfavorable. If nothing changes, by 2050, the median age may be 52 (it will be 35 in the U.S.). With a population that is not only aging but shrinking, Europe will have to accept increasing numbers of immigrants (which is politically difficult) or accept that being older and smaller will diminish its influence in world affairs. As one demographer put it, the Europeans are "aging in a world that is becoming younger. And in a global economy, they're not going to share in the energy and vitality that comes with a younger population."[16]

At the same time, many European domestic policies appeal to young populations in modern democracies. For example, European policies on capital punishment, gun control, climate change, and the rights of homosexuals are probably closer to the views of many younger people in rich countries around the world than are American government policies. The new constitution of South Africa bears more resemblance to the European Convention on Human Rights than to the American Bill of Rights. The First Amendment expert Fred Schauer points out, "On issues of freedom of speech, freedom of the press, and equality, for example, the United States is seen as representing an extreme position, whether it be in the degree of its legal protection of press misbehavior and of racist and other forms of hateful speech or in its unwillingness to treat race-based affirmative action as explicitly constitutionally permissible."[17] It is also interesting that European precedents are now being cited in American law. When the American Supreme Court decided the case of *Lawrence v. Texas* regarding sexual privacy in 2003, the majority opinion cited a 1981 decision of the European Court of Human Rights for the first time.

On economic policies as well, though many people admire the success of the American economy, not all extol it as a model for other countries. Some prefer the European approach, in which government plays a greater role in the economy than it does in the United States. Social safety nets and unions are stronger and labor markets more regulated in Europe. American cultural attitudes, bankruptcy laws, and financial structures more strongly favor entrepreneurs than do European ones, but many people in Europe object to the price of high levels of inequality and insecurity that accompany America's greater reliance on market forces. America does better than Europe in job creation, with less than half the rate of unemployment in Germany, but *The Economist* concludes that "the notion that the American economy stands on top of the world is questionable. It is also vulnerable to criticism because of its wider income inequality."[18] The lowest 10 percent of people in America's income distribution were only thirteenth from the bottom in average income when compared with relatively poor people in other advanced economies. Many Europeans ranked higher. The superior job performance of the American economy does not alone make it more attractive than Europe's.[19] For example, in the 1991 poll cited earlier, majorities in Poland, Czechoslovakia, Hungary, and Bulgaria said a social democracy along the lines of Sweden was most appropriate for their countries.[20]

In addition to its attractive culture and domestic policies, Europe also derives soft power from its foreign policies, which often contribute to global public goods. Of course not all European policies are far-sighted—witness its protectionist common agricultural policy, which damages farmers in poor countries—but Europe gains credibility from its positions on global climate change, international law, and human rights treaties. Moreover, Europeans provide 70 percent of overseas development assistance to poor countries—four times more than the United States. Europe also has ten times as many troops as the United States involved in peacekeeping operations under multilateral organizations such as the UN and NATO.[21] France took the lead recently in sending a mission to the

Congo. In 2003, France and Germany had more than twice as many troops in Kosovo as the United States, and Europeans working through NATO took charge of the International Security Force in Afghanistan.

Europeans have been less likely to shrink from the hard tasks of nation building that America initially eschewed under the Bush administration. In many ways, Europeans are more adept and comfortable than the United States in deploying the civilian resources that enhance soft power. British Foreign Secretary Jack Straw has argued, "Europe's experience in the exercise of the subtle art of soft power could prove indispensable to the reconstruction of Iraq. The EU tends to exert its influence overseas via the promotion of democracy and development through trade and aid. The results have been impressive in central and eastern Europe."[22]

In recent years Europeans have also been more comfortable with and adept at using multilateral institutions than Americans. This is in part a reflection of their experiences in the development of the European Union and in part a reflection of their self-interest in seeking multilateral constraints on the world's only superpower. But whatever the reasons, in a world where unilateralism is heavily criticized, the European propensity toward multilateralism makes European countries' policies attractive to many other countries. Europeans have used their soft power in multilateral institutions to deprive the United States of the legitimizing effects of such support. As we saw in chapter 1, France was able to create a coalition that countered American soft power by preventing a second Security Council resolution before the Iraq War. As the political analyst Andrew Moravscik points out, "In country after country, polls have shown that a second United Nations Security Council resolution would have given public opinion a 30–40 per cent swing towards military action."[23] Instead, the United States had to pay a higher price than necessary for the war both in soft power and in the subsequent costs of policing and reconstructing Iraq.

The European preference for multilateral cooperation has generated a few successes that have increased Europe's soft power as well as its economic power. After a bumpy start, the Airbus consortium surpassed Boeing as the world's leading manufacturer of commercial jetliners. In the mobile phone industry, European governments agreed on a single regulatory standard, GSM, as early as 1987, while Americans used a market-driven approach to allow a standard to emerge and dominate. The result was that Europe developed a stronger infrastructure than the United States and was able to dominate the wireless market in the 1990s.[24] A future test of the European approach will be the Galileo global navigation satellite system, Europe's answer to the U.S.-based Global Positioning System (GPS). While excessive bureaucracy can hamper the European approach, the ability to work cooperatively on large information infrastructure projects that serve as global public goods can increase Europe's soft power as well as its economic power.

Europeans also invest more in their public diplomacy, as we shall see in the next chapter. The Europeans have a longer tradition and spend more, particularly in international cultural relations, an area in which France had the highest per capita spending, over $17 and more than four times that of second-ranked Canada; Britain and Sweden rank third and fourth. In comparison, American State Department funding for international cultural programs spending was only 65 cents per capita.[25] In addition, European countries have been increasing their efforts to recruit students to their schools and universities from other parts of the world.

Not only can European soft power be used to counter American soft power and raise the price of unilateral actions, but it can also be a source of assistance and reinforcement for American soft power and increase the likelihood of the United States' achieving its objectives. Soft power can be shared and used in a cooperative fashion. European promotion of democracy and human rights helps advance shared values that are consistent with American objectives. The Islamist extremists of Al Qaeda are fighting against Western values, not just American values, and European public diplomacy that counters their appeal is beneficial to the United States.

French political leaders have often talked about creating a multi-polar balance of power, but many Europeans see such dreams as unrealistic in the current world situation. Most Europeans realize that multilateral diplomacy is possible even without a multipolar military balance, and they would be happy to share their soft power with the United States if we would be more consultative in our approach. As a sympathetic British observer put the point during the Iraq war, "Maddening contradictions have all along been at the heart of the willful destruction of the international security system during the past few months. The U.S. quest for untrammeled primacy is doomed. America's security and prosperity depend on its political influence as much as on its military might. The U.S. has been strong because it has been admired."[26] In other words, the extent to which the growth of European soft power is an asset or a liability for the United States depends upon American policies and rests very much on America's own choices. European soft power can be used to help or hurt the United States, depending on how America behaves.

ASIA

Asian countries also have impressive potential resources for soft power. The arts, fashion, and cuisine of Asia's ancient cultures have already had a strong impact on other parts of the world for centuries. But Asia also went through a period of relative decline as it lagged behind Western nations that went through the industrial revolution, and that cut into its influence. The Asian Development Bank has calculated that in 1820, at the beginning of the industrial age, Asia made up an estimated three-fifths of world product. By 1940, this had fallen to one-fifth, even though the region was home to three-fifths of world population. Rapid economic growth has brought that back to two-fifths today, and the bank speculates that Asia could return to its historical levels by 2025.[27] In the last two decades of the twentieth century, China, Asia's largest country, had high annual growth rates of 7 to 9 percent that led to a remarkable tripling of its GNP and enhanced its reputation and soft power. Nonetheless, even China has a long way to go, and faces many obstacles to its development. At the beginning of the twenty-first century, the American economy was more than twice the size of China's. And, as a Singapore columnist observed, "When it comes to soft power, it will take much longer before it can make an impact close to what the U.S. enjoys now."[28]

In the 1950s, the mention of Asia conjured up images of poverty and starvation. There was a brief political infatuation among some in the West in the 1960s with Nehru jackets and Maoist revolution, but it was relatively brief. As John Lennon sang at the height of the antiwar movement, "If you go carrying pictures of Chairman Mao, you're not going to make it with anyone anyhow."[29] The real resurgence of Asia began with the economic success of Japan. Asians often refer to the image of geese flying in formation to describe the way that smaller countries like Singapore, South Korea, Malaysia, and others closely followed Japan's strategy of targeting strategic industries for development, financing major projects, exporting fiercely, and protecting infant industries. One of Malaysia's economic planners has noted, "Japan's experience of rebuilding after the war, the way it got workers and management to cooperate and got the economy to grow in leaps and bounds, seems very Asian to us. It has much more relevance to our society than the experience of the West."[30] Japan's personal income increased from 20 percent of the U.S. level in 1950 to 75 percent by the end of the century, a remarkable performance that not only made Japanese wealthy but also enhanced the country's soft power.

The Asian economic miracle helped support an ideology of Asian values that was often a convenient excuse for authoritarian leaders to maintain political stability. For example, Malaysia, Singapore, and Indonesia resisted pressure for more democracy and human rights on the grounds that the West was trying to impose alien values that favor individual rights on an ancient culture where the highest value is placed on the welfare of society as a whole. Asian values became an assertion of regional identity by nations that had begun to flex their economic muscle and to develop their own polit-ical systems.[31] But after the Asian economic crisis of 1997 and the consequent slowdown of growth in many countries in the region, other voices began to be heard. The *New York Times* reported, "To-day, there is a slow, daily tug of war between the old-guard tradition-alists—the former Asian values crowd—and the insurgents of an open society, who are developing a sort of indigenous version of Western values."[32] Asian corporate models rested heavily on family relationships and connections to government that were opaque to outsiders. But, as *The Economist* observed, that "opacity costs money, as untrusting foreign investors demand bigger returns. And all Asian countries crave the cloak of international respectability from mem-bership of the OECD club to the kudos of hosting the Olympic Games or World Cup."[33] The Asian economic miracle was real and for a time generated soft power for the successful countries, but when it ran into trouble in the 1990s, it lost the clout to sustain the myth that it supported or resulted from Asian values.

Japan has more potential soft power resources than any other Asian country. It is the first non-Western country that was able to fully modernize to the point of equality with the West in income and technology while showing that it is possible to maintain a unique culture. Today Japan ranks . . .

✻ . . . first in the world in number of patents
✻ . . . third in expenditure on research and development as a percent of gross domestic product
✻ . . . third in international air travel
✻ . . . second in book sales and music sales
✻ . . . second in the number of Internet hosts
✻ . . . second in high-tech exports
✻ . . . first in development assistance
✻ . . . first for life expectancy[34]

Japan is home to three of the top 25 multinational brand names, Toyota, Honda, and Sony.[35] In the 1980s Japan derived considerable soft power from its manufacturing prowess. The writer Douglas McGray observed, "Seeking guidance on everything from 'quality circles' to 'just in time' inventory management, U.S. corporate executives bought stacks of books on Japanese management techniques."[36]

The decade-long economic slowdown of the 1990s tarnished Japan's reputation for economic prowess, but it did not erase the nation's soft-power resources. "Instead of collapsing beneath its political and economic misfortunes," writes McGray, "Japan's global cultural influence has only grown. In fact, from pop music to consumer electronics, architecture to fashion, and food to art, Japan has far greater cultural influence now than it did in the 1980s when it was an economic superpower."[37] Japanese manufacturers rule the roost in home video games. Japanese images dominated children's dreams quite handily over the last five years with their mix of cuteness and power. Pokémon cartoons are broadcast in 65 countries, and Japanese animation is a huge hit with American filmmakers and teenagers. Its style has spilled over into American design trends as well.[38] Japan's popular culture was still producing potential soft-power resources even after its economy slowed down.

Japanese cultural attraction is not limited to its pop culture. Japan's traditional arts, design, and cuisine have long found followers outside the country. Authors like Nobel Prize–winning Kenzaburo Oe have wide international audiences. In film, Akira Kurosawa is considered one of the great directors of all time. In classical music, Seiji Ozawa, the former director of the Boston Symphony, is widely renowned. Japan also benefits from the cultural attractiveness of its traditional spiritual disciplines such as Zen Buddhism and the martial arts.

But there are also limits to Japan's soft power. Unlike Germany, which repudiated its past aggression and reconciled with its neighbors in the framework of the European Union, Japan has never fully come to terms with its record of foreign aggression in the 1930s.

The residual suspicion that lingers in countries such as China and Korea sets limits on Japan's soft power. Japan does not have the full admiration of its Asian neighbors. A 1996 Japanese poll that asked which features of Japanese culture were attractive found that 72 percent of Chinese were interested in Japanese household appliances and 61 percent in its style of business management, but only 11 percent in Japanese television, 5 percent in Japanese music, and 7 percent in the Japanese lifestyle.[39] Similarly, a 2001 *Newsweek* poll found that where 65 percent of Americans found Japan "admirable" and only 27 percent thought the Japanese "arrogant," a mere 34 percent of South Koreans found Japan admirable and 59 percent considered the Japanese arrogant.[40]

Like Europe, Japan faces serious demographic challenges. By the middle of the twenty-first century Japan's population could shrink by 30 percent unless it attracts 17 million immigrants, a difficult task in a country that has been historically resistant to immigration. Moreover, the Japanese language is not widely spoken, and Japan's English language skills, according to one journalist, rank "among the worst in Asia, making it difficult to attract international talent to its universities."[41] A recent Japanese prime minister's commission on the nation's goals in the twenty-first century called for a new reinvention of Japan.[42] Given the weakness of the political process, the need for further deregulation, the aging of the population, and the resistance to immigration, such change will not be easy and may take more than a decade to complete.[43] But given Japan's past record of twice reinventing itself—after the Meiji revolution in the nineteenth century and after World War II—plus the undiminished skills of Japan's people, the stability of its society, areas of technological leadership (for instance, mobile Internet applications), and manufacturing skills, it is not impossible.

A decade ago some observers thought the close collaboration of government and industry in Japan would give it a lead in soft power in the information age. Japan could develop an ability to manipulate perceptions worldwide instantaneously and "destroy those that impede Japanese economic prosperity and cultural acceptance."[44]

When Matsushita purchased the American motion picture company MCA, its president said that movies critical of Japan would not be produced.[45] Japanese media tried to break into world markets, and the government-owned NHK network began satellite broadcasts in English. The venture failed, however, as NHK's reports seemed to lag behind those of commercial news organizations, and the network had to rely on CNN and ABC for content.[46] This does not mean that Japan lacks soft-power resources.[47] But Japan's culture remains much more inward-oriented than that of the U.S., and its government's unwillingness to deal frankly with the history of the 1930s continues to limit its ability to transform those resources into soft power in the sense of obtaining the policy outcomes it desires.

Further in the future, China and India loom as the giants of Asia, and there are already signs of the expansion of their soft-power resources. In 2000, the Chinese novelist Gao Xingjian won China's first Nobel Prize for literature, followed a year later by the Indian diaspora writer V. S. Naipaul. In June 1997, *The New Yorker* devoted an entire issue to fiction by Indian writers. The Chinese film *Crouching Tiger, Hidden Dragon* became the highest-grossing non-English-language film, and Indian movies like *Monsoon Wedding* were box-office successes in the U.S.[48] Yao Ming, the Chinese star of the National Basketball Association's Houston Rockets, could become another Michael Jordan, and China is set to host the 2008 Summer Olympics. China's investment in manned space flight also helps to increase its prestige and attraction. Large expatriate communities in the United States—2.4 million Chinese and 1.7 million Indians— have increased interest in their home countries among Americans. Moreover, the transnational connections in the information industry are close, as U.S. high-tech companies increasingly employ affiliates in Bangalore or Chennai to provide real-time services here.

But the real promise for China and India still lies in the future. Rapid economic growth is likely to increase both countries' hard and soft power, but at this point, neither country ranks high on the various indices of potential soft-power resources that are possessed by the United States, Europe, and Japan. While culture provides some soft power, domestic policies and values set limits, particularly in China, where the Communist Party fears allowing too much intellectual freedom and resists outside influences. Both countries have a reputation for major corruption in government. India benefits from democratic politics, but still suffers from overly bureaucratized government. And the recent revival of Hindu extremism and the killing of Muslims in Gujarat has tarnished its democratic reputation. In foreign policy as well, both countries' reputations are burdened with the problems of longstanding conflicts, over Taiwan and Kashmir, respectively. Moreover, in the United States the attraction of an authoritarian China is limited by the concern that it could become a threat sometime in the future. The soft power of Asian countries is likely to increase in the future, but at this stage they lag in soft-power resources behind the United States and Europe.

Of course smaller countries both in Asia and other regions also enjoy soft power. South Korea and Thailand attract others through their economic and democratic progress. Thailand has even discovered that foreigners love Thai food, and its government set a goal of boosting the number of Thai restaurants overseas as a way to "subtly help to deepen relations with other countries."[49] Soft power is available to all countries, and many invest in ways to use soft-power resources to "punch above their weight" in international politics. As we saw in chapter 1, Norway has enhanced its attractiveness by clever policies even while remaining outside the EU. And for decades the most trusted countries in Europe have been the small countries of Switzerland, Scandinavia, and the Benelux group.[50] For many countries, the constitutional ideas of Canada "have been disproportionately influential, perhaps more influential than those of the United States."[51] South Africa is widely admired for its progress in overcoming racial apartheid peacefully, and Brazil projects a certain attraction both from its vibrant culture and its promise in the future. Even if they do not have the overall power resources to match the largest countries, smaller or less powerful countries still can present challenges greater than their military size would imply. And not only states can pose such challenges.

NONSTATE ACTORS

The information age has been marked by an increasingly important role of nonstate actors on the international stage. Private organizations increasingly cross national boundaries. This is not totally new, but the information revolution has led to a dramatic increase in scale in recent years, with the number of NGOs (nongovernmental organizations) increasing from 6,000 to approximately 26,000 during the 1990s alone. And the numbers do not tell the full story, because they represent only formally constituted organizations.[52]

Many nongovernmental organizations claim to act as a "global conscience" representing broad public interests beyond the purview of individual states. They develop new norms directly by pressing governments and business leaders to change policies, and indirectly by altering public perceptions of what governments and firms should be doing. In terms of power resources, these new groups rarely possess much hard power (although it is worth noting that the budget of Greenpeace in 2001 was $157 million, compared to the $90 million budget of the intergovernmental World Trade Organization). In any event, the information revolution has greatly enhanced NGOs' soft power.[53] Because they are able to attract followers, governments have to take NGOs into account as both allies and adversaries. From the American point of view, it is worth noting that Brussels, London, and Paris rank ahead of Washington and New York as host cities for international nongovernmental organizations.[54]

Not only the number of transnational contacts but also the number of *types* of these organizations has increased. A few decades ago, large bureaucratic organizations with hefty budgets like multinational corporations or the Roman Catholic church were the most typical type of transnational organization. The soft power of corporate brand names has been familiar for decades. Such organizations remain important, but the reduced cost of communication in the Internet era has opened the field to loosely structured network organizations with little headquarters staff, and even to individuals. This is part of the democratization of technology that we discussed in chapter 1. These flexible nongovernmental organizations and networks are particularly effective in penetrating states without regard to borders. Because they often involve citizens who are well placed in the domestic politics of several countries, such networks are able to focus the attention of the media and governments on their issues. They create a new type of transnational political coalitions. For example, the coalition to ban land mines brought together NGOs, celebrities, and politicians in many countries.

The information revolution makes states more porous. Governments now have to share the stage with actors who can use information to enhance their soft power and press governments directly, or indirectly by mobilizing their publics. Given the power of credible editors and cue givers who can cut through the avalanche of available information in the Internet age, a rough way to gauge the increasing importance of transnational organizations is to look at the number of mentions that these organizations receive in mainstream media publications. By this measure, the biggest NGOs have become established players in the battle for the attention of influential editors. For example, after Human Rights Watch released its *2003 World Report*, which included strong criticism of the U.S. government for its conduct in the war on terrorism, articles appeared in 288 newspaper and magazines over the next ten days mentioning the organization.[55]

News coverage over the past decade has reflected the growth of this general sector; the use of the term "nongovernmental organization" or "NGO" has increased 17-fold since 1992. Not only Human Rights Watch but also other NGOs such as Amnesty International, the International Red Cross, Greenpeace, Doctors without Borders (Médecins Sans Frontières), and Transparency International have undergone exponential growth in the number of their mainstream media mentions.

In the information age, governments that want to see rapid economic growth find that they can no longer maintain the barriers to information flows that historically protected officials from outside scrutiny. Even large countries with hard power, such as the United States, are affected. For example, a campaign by NGOs helped to scuttle a proposed Multilateral Agreement on Investment in the late 1990s, and NGOs used the Internet to plan the disruption of the World Trade Organization summit in 1999 that became known as the "battle of Seattle." The Pentagon opposed a treaty banning landmines, but a mixed coalition of Internet-based organizations working with middle-power governments such as Canada and individual politicians and celebrities such as Princess Diana was able to bring the treaty into existence in 1997. Another example is the Framework Convention on Tobacco Control that was ratified in May 2003 by the 192 members of the World Health Organization. The United States initially had strong objections to the treaty but dropped them in the face of international criticism.[56]

A fascinating use of the Internet to wield soft power can be found in the politics of diaspora communities. David Bollier, an expert on the impact of digital technologies, notes, "The Internet has been a godsend to such populations because it enables large numbers of geographically isolated people with a shared history to organize into large virtual communities."[57] The Internet enables them to present attractive alternative ideas to those back home. Internet connections between foreign nationals and local citizens helped to spark protests in Beijing against anti-Chinese riots taking place in Indonesia in 1998. The frustration of ethnic Chinese living in Indonesia was transferred to Beijing with remarkable speed. Similarly, in Zimbabwe, the Internet was crucial in spreading news about government actions during disputed elections.

One example of a diaspora group that has effectively used the Internet and other media sources to affect political outcomes in its home country is the Ghanaian expatriate community. In the elections of 2000, the first real opportunity for Ghanaians to change their government through democratic means, the diaspora network was crucial in mobilizing support and money for the opposition candidate. Online community networks such as the Ghana Cybergroup (GCG), established in 1999 in New York, mobilized the diaspora in the United States to aggressively campaign for regime change in Ghana. In 2000, GCG members were encouraged to "find every means (email, phone, etc) to communicate with their families at home to go out and vote" in the national elections. And now the GCG has refocused its mission on attracting development assistance for Ghana, and is in the process of establishing a network among the 2.5 million Ghanaian expatriates to increase the flow of capital to their home country.[58]

Transnational corporations often are the target of NGO activities such as campaigns to "name and shame" companies that pay low wages to laborers in poor countries. Such campaigns sometimes succeed because they can credibly threaten to deprive the corporations of the soft power of their valuable global brand names. When Shell proposed deep-ocean disposal of its Brent Spar drilling rig, which allegedly would have polluted the ocean, Greenpeace organized a boycott campaign that forced Shell to opt for more costly dismantling on shore. Ironically, when it was later disclosed that the original Shell proposal was better for the environment, Greenpeace's reputation and soft power suffered. In any event, Shell decided that it had to increase its attention to NGOs: the company also recently announced that it would not drill in any spots designated UNESCO World Heritage sites. This decision came two years after Shell acceded to pressure from environmentalists and scrapped plans to drill in a World Heritage site in Bangladesh.[59] Transnational drug companies were shamed by NGOs into giving up lawsuits in South Africa in 2002 over infringements of their patents on AIDS drugs because, the *Financial Times* reported, "demands for greater social responsibility from business are getting louder, better organized and more popular." Similar campaigns of naming and shaming have affected the investment and employment patterns of Mattel, Nike, and a host of other companies.

NGOs vary enormously in their organization, budgets, the accountability to their members, and their sense of responsibility for the accuracy of their claims. Their soft power varies accordingly. While some NGOs are more credible and trusted than governments, others are not. Overall, a recent poll in Europe found that 42 percent of Europeans tended to trust NGOs whereas 36 percent expressed distrust. In Britain and Germany, however, the number of those who distrusted NGOs exceeded those who trusted them.[60] Thus it is hyperbole when activists call such organizations "the world's other superpower," but at the same time, governments ignore them at their peril. Some have reputations and credibility that give them impressive domestic as well as international political clout. Others may lack credibility among moderate citizens, but have organizational and communication skills that allow them to mobilize demonstrations that governments cannot ignore. Few international meetings can be planned today without consideration of the prospect of demonstrations. For better and for worse, NGOs and network organizations have soft-power resources and do not hesitate to use them.

For centuries, organized religious movements have possessed soft power. The Roman Catholic church is organized on a global scale, and many Catholics around the world adhere to its teachings on issues like birth control and abortion because of attraction, not coercion. Other religious organizations—among them Protestant, Islamic, and Buddhist—have extensive missionary efforts that have attracted millions of people to adhere to their teachings, particularly in Latin America and Africa in recent decades. But as we saw in the last chapter, intolerant religious organizations can repel as well as attract. In some circumstances aggressive proselytizing can destroy rather than create soft power.

Intergovernmental organizations such as the United Nations or the World Trade Organization can also develop soft power. Strictly speaking, they are the creatures of the states that formed them, but the diplomacy within different organizations takes on characteristics that reflect the unique procedures and culture of the organization. Thus, for example, the reputation of the United Nations cannot be understood without contrasting the roles of the General Assembly (with its rhetoric) and the Security Council (with its vetoes), as well as the deference to regional caucuses that produces damaging aberrations such as Libya's chairing the Human Rights Commission. The personality and skill of the secretary-general can also affect the reputation of the organization. Like the pope, Kofi Annan commands few troops, but his popularity and position assure attention to his statements.

The UN is not the only source of legitimacy in world politics, but its universality, legal framework, and relative attractiveness do give its votes and pronouncements a considerable degree of legitimacy. The UN's reputation, and thus its soft power, is susceptible to changing political events. For example, the American decision to enter the Iraq War without a second Security Council resolution hurt the UN's as well as America's reputation and led majorities in 19 of 21 countries polled to say that the UN was no longer as important as it had been in dealing with international conflicts.[61] On the other hand, over two-thirds in the U.S. and European populations still rate the UN favorably after the war.[62] The overall reputation of the UN has fluctuated over the years. In Europe, post–Iraq War trust in the UN is below the trust level of 2002, but it remains comparable to the 1990s. In the United States, overall favorable ratings for the UN have rebounded to prewar levels after a brief dip. The UN's job approval rating in the United States was actually lower in the 1980s than before the Iraq War (28 percent in August 1985; 38 percent in March 2003) and hit its historic low during the Korean War (23 percent in May 1951).[63] The attractiveness and soft-power resources of the UN vary over time and have limits, but governments cannot afford to ignore it without paying a price.

Soft power can also adhere to malevolent organizations and networks. Soft power depends on a receptive audience even if the eye of the beholder is evil. Transnational terrorist organizations like Al Qaeda may be repulsive to the majority of the world, but they are clearly attractive to some extremists. If the Soviet Union and Communism presented the most dangerous soft-power challenges to the United States in the Cold War era, today's greatest challenge comes from radical Islamist ideology and organizations. In particular, the fundamentalist Wahhabi sect, which originated on the Arabian peninsula in the eighteenth century, has been augmented by radical outgrowths of the Muslim Brotherhood movement, which arose in Egypt in the 1920s. Ironically, Sayyid Quttb, a key intellectual figure for radical Islamists, was a Muslim Brother who lived for a short time in the United States and was disgusted by what he considered the meaninglessness of American life.[64] As noted before, culture that is attractive to many can be repulsive to some.

The rise of radical Islamism received a good deal of state help from Saudi Arabia, where the ruling family agreed to propagate Wahhabism as a means of propitiating the clerics, thus buying "their own political legitimacy at the cost of stability elsewhere."[65] Because funding of Wahhabist institutions comes from both Saudi government ministries and private charities, it is virtually impossible to estimate the total spending. One expert testified to Congress that the Saudis had spent roughly $70 billion on aid projects since the 1970s, and others report that they sponsored 1,500 mosques and 2,000 schools worldwide from Indonesia to France.[66] These institutions often displace more moderate and worse-funded institutions promulgating moderate interpretations of Islam.[67] Even if these numbers are incorrect, a fraction of the dollar figures still dwarfs what the United States has spent on public diplomacy in the Muslim world.

Ironically, the soft power of Wahhabism has not proved to be a resource that the Saudi government could control or use to obtain favorable outcomes. Instead, it has been like a sorcerer's apprentice that has come back to bedevil its original creator. The radicals regard the royal family as corrupt and in league with Western infidels. They aim to overthrow or disrupt the government, and launched terrorist attacks in Riyadh in 2003. The royal family's bargain with the Wahhabist clerics has backfired because the soft power of Islamic radicalism has flowed in the direction of Osama bin Laden and his goal of overthrowing the Saudi government, not in the direction of making the Saudi government more secure.

A snapshot of this situation was captured by a poll taken in a number of predominantly Muslim countries shortly after the Iraq War. Pluralities in Indonesia, Jordan, Pakistan, Morocco, and the

Palestinian Authority said they had a lot or some confidence in Osama bin Laden to do the right thing regarding world affairs. In those same countries, vast majorities had more confidence in bin Laden than in George W. Bush or Tony Blair. Although it is not surprising that many Muslims had negative feelings about Bush and Blair in the aftermath of a war against a Muslim country, the fact that bin Laden inspired confidence sent a clear message to Americans about the soft power of its sworn enemy. Similar anecdotal evidence abounded in the fall of 2001 in the aftermath of 9/11, when reports came from Africa that "Osama" was now a popular name for baby boys, and from Pakistan, where bin Laden T-shirts were selling well. In part this may be a new twist in the long tradition of Robin Hood legends among the poor and disenfranchised, but it also represents deeper trends in Islamic opinion. Because the war on terrorism involves a civil war between radicals and moderates within Islamic civilization, the soft power of the Islamists is a disturbing symptom and a warning of the need for Americans and others to find better ways of projecting soft power to strengthen the moderates. Moderate churches and synagogues can play a role with moderate Muslims. In all three religions the prophet Abraham is a revered figure, and so the idea of an Abrahamic dialogue among Muslims, Christians, and Jews may be an example of the ways that nongovernmental actors can exercise their soft power and create bridges of understanding.

THE UNITED STATES is the world's only military superpower. It also remains the world's mightiest country in terms of economic and soft power, but America is not nearly as dominant in these two domains of power as in the military domain. The trends of the information age and the spread of democratization should benefit American soft power in the future, but they will also benefit Europe and other countries that are able to adapt to the new conditions. More problematically, the trends of the information age will increase the soft power of nonstate actors, both good and bad. To cope with a world in which the soft power of others is increasing, the United States will have to invest more in its own soft-power resources, and learn to wield its soft power more effectively.

CHAPTER FOUR

Wielding Soft Power

GOVERNMENTS USE MILITARY POWER to issue threats, fight, and, with a combination of skill and luck, achieve desired outcomes within a reasonable time. Economic power is often a similarly straightforward matter. Governments can freeze foreign bank accounts overnight, and can distribute bribes or aid promptly (although economic sanctions often take a long time, if ever, to produce desired outcomes). Soft power is more difficult to wield, because, as we saw in chapter 1, many of its crucial resources are outside the control of governments, and their effects depend heavily on acceptance by the receiving audiences. Moreover, soft-power resources often work indirectly by shaping the environment for policy, and sometimes take years to produce the desired outcomes.

Of course, these differences are matters of degree. Not all wars or economic actions promptly produce desired outcomes—witness the length and ultimate failure of the Vietnam War, or the fact that economic sanctions have historically produced their intended outcomes in only about a third of the cases where they were tried.[1] In Iraq, Saddam Hussein survived sanctions for more than a decade, and although the four-week American military campaign broke his regime, it was only a first step toward achieving American objectives in Iraq. As one former military officer has observed, the mark of a great campaign is not what it destroys, but what it creates, and on that question the jury will remain out for a number of years on the Iraq War.[2] Moreover, sometimes dissemination of information can quickly produce or prevent a desired outcome. Generally, however, soft-power resources are slower, more diffuse, and more cumbersome to wield than hard-power resources.

EARLY EFFORTS

The fact that soft-power resources are awkward to wield has not prevented governments from trying. Take France for example. In the seventeenth and eighteenth centuries, France promoted its culture throughout Europe. French not only became the language of diplomacy but was even used at some foreign courts, such as those of Prussia and Russia. During the French Revolution, France sought to go over the heads of foreign governments and appeal directly to their countries' populations by promoting its revolutionary ideology. After its defeat in the Franco-Prussian War, the French government sought to repair the nation's shattered prestige by promoting its language and literature through the Alliance Française, which was created in 1883. As the historian Richard Pells noted, "The projection of French culture abroad thus became a significant component of French diplomacy."[3] Italy, Germany, and others soon followed suit by founding institutes to promote their cultures overseas.

The outbreak of World War I saw a rapid acceleration of efforts to deploy soft power, as most of the governments established offices to propagandize their cause. The United States not only established its own office but also during the early years before American entry into the war was a central target of other countries' efforts, as Britain and Germany competed to create favorable images in American public opinion. Noticing the counterproductive effects of German mass propaganda, Britain was more successful by focusing on American elites and using a soft sell. One early academic study of wartime propaganda reported, "The sheer radiation of aristocratic distinction was enough to warm the cockles of many a staunch Republican heart, and to evoke enthusiasm for the country which could produce such dignity, elegance and affability."[4]

The United States was a relative latecomer to the idea of using information and culture for the purposes of diplomacy. In 1917, President Woodrow Wilson established the Committee on Public Information, which was directed by his friend the newspaperman George Creel. Creel's task, he said, was "a vast enterprise in salesmanship, the world's greatest adventure in advertising."[5] Creel insisted that his office's activities did not constitute propaganda and were merely educational and informative. But the facts belied his denials. Among other things, Creel organized tours, churned out pamphlets on "the Gospel of Americanism," established a government-run news service, made sure that motion picture producers received wartime allotments of scarce materials, and saw to it that the films portrayed America in a positive light.[6] The Committee on Public Information aroused sufficient suspicions in Congress and the American people that it was abolished shortly after the return of peace.

The advent of radio in the 1920s led many governments into the arena of foreign-language broadcasting, and in the 1930s, Communists in the Soviet Union and Fascists in Germany and Italy competed to promote favorable images of their countries and ideologies to foreign publics. In addition to its foreign-language radio broadcasts, Nazi Germany perfected the propaganda film. In 1937, Britain's foreign secretary, Anthony Eden, realized about the new communications, "It is perfectly true, of course, that good cultural propaganda cannot remedy the damage done by a bad foreign policy, but it is no exaggeration to say that even the best of diplomatic policies may fail if it neglects the task of interpretation and persuasion which modern conditions impose."[7] By the end of the decade, the BBC, founded in 1922, was broadcasting in all major European languages as well as Arabic.

In the late 1930s, the Roosevelt administration became convinced that "America's security depended on its ability to speak to and to win the support of people in other countries."[8] President Roosevelt was particularly concerned about German propaganda in

Latin America. In 1938, the State Department established the Division of Cultural Relations, and supplemented it two years later with the Office of Inter-American Affairs, under Nelson Rockefeller, which actively promoted American information and culture in Latin America. In 1939, Germany beamed 7 hours of programming a week to Latin America, and the United States, about 12. By 1941, the United States was broadcasting around the clock.[9]

After America's entry into the war, the government's cultural offensive became global in scope. In 1942 Roosevelt created the Office of Wartime Information (OWI) to deal in presumably accurate information, while an intelligence organization, the Office of Strategic Services (OSS), included dissemination of disinformation among its functions. The OWI even worked to shape Hollywood's products into effective propaganda tools, suggesting additions and deletions to films and denying licenses to others.[10] And Hollywood executives, motivated by a mixture of patriotism and self-interest, were happy to cooperate. Well before the Cold War, according to Richard Pells, "American corporate and advertising executives, as well as the heads of Hollywood studios, were selling not only their products but also America's culture and values, the secrets of its success, to the rest of the world."[11] Wartime soft-power resources were created in part by the government and in part independently.

Radio played a significant role. What became known as the Voice of America grew rapidly during World War II. Modeled on the BBC's approach, by 1943 it had 23 transmitters delivering news in 27 languages. After the war, with the start of the Cold War and the growth of the Soviet threat, the VOA continued to expand, but so did a debate about how much it should be a captive purveyor of government information or an independent representative of American culture. Special radio stations were added such as Radio Liberty and Radio Free Europe, which used exiles to broadcast to the Eastern bloc. More generally, as the Cold War developed, there was a division between those who favored the slow media of cultural diplomacy—art, books, exchanges—that had a trickle-down effect, and those who favored the fast information media of radio, movies, and newsreels, which promised more immediate and visible "bang for the buck."[12]

Throughout the Cold War proponents of these two approaches struggled over how the government should invest in soft power. The "tough-minded" did not shy away from direct propaganda while the "tender-minded" argued that changing foreign attitudes is a gradual process that needs to be measured in years.[13] There were also struggles over how free of government control government-supported programs should be. In the end, according to Reinhold Wagnleitner, American foreign cultural programs were "sucked into the vortex of an aggressive anti-Communist foreign policy." For example, a directive at the time stated that our overseas libraries "have to be objective, but on the other hand, the very definition of our libraries is that they are special purpose libraries. The best we can hope to do is to achieve and maintain the illusion of objectivity."[14] There was a thin line between information and propaganda. Henry James, Jr., a State Department official, noted that the inclusion of magazines critical of the Truman administration and books on racial questions impressed readers abroad with the "credibility of the material." Attacks by Senator Joseph McCarthy produced a brief period of hysteria and censorship, but new directives in 1953 restored more balance.[15]

These struggles persisted despite various reorganizations of American institutions for public diplomacy over the years. The debate over how directly or indirectly the government should try to control its instruments of soft power can never be fully resolved because both sides make valid points. For 46 years after 1953, the central institution of public diplomacy was the United States Information Agency (USIA). The Voice of America was folded into it in 1978, and in the 1980s, the Reagan Administration tried to make both institutions more directly responsive to the government's immediate objectives.[16] In 1999, USIA was abolished and its functions were absorbed into the State Department, where it would be closer to policy centers, while VOA and other specialized stations were put under a new bipartisan entity, the Broadcasting Board of

Governors. Currently, the VOA broadcasts in 53 languages to an estimated audience of 91 million people.[17]

More important than the vicissitudes of reorganization was the low priority assigned to soft power in the postwar era. True, President Eisenhower said in retirement that he should have taken money out of the military budget to strengthen USIA, but that was not typical. One observer noted, "No president, with the possible exception of Dwight Eisenhower, has considered the director of USIA important. In the Cuban Missile Crisis, [USIA director Edward R.] Murrow was not involved. He coined the phrase that he wanted to be in on the takeoff, not on the crash landing."[18] Even in the midst of the Cold War in the seventies, France and Germany spent more on policy information and cultural communication functions than did the United States—in absolute terms—and Britain and Japan spent more as a percent of their budgets, .23 and .14 percent, respectively, compared to the United States' .11 percent. In 1975, the "leader of the free world" ranked fifth among the key Western allies in government investment in soft-power resources.[19]

With the end of the Cold War, Americans were more interested in budget savings than in investments in soft power. From 1963 to 1993, the federal budget grew 15-fold, but the USIA budget grew only 6.5 times. USIA had over 12,000 employees at its peak in the mid-sixties, but only 9,000 in 1994 and 6,715 on the eve of its takeover by the State Department.[20] Soft power seemed expendable. Between 1989 and 1999, the budget of USIA, adjusted for inflation, decreased 10 percent. While government-funded radio broadcasts reached half the Soviet population every week and between 70 and 80 percent of the populace of Eastern Europe during the Cold War, at the beginning of the new century, a mere 2 percent of Arabs heard the VOA.[21] Resources for the USIA mission in Indonesia, the world's largest Muslim nation, were cut in half. From 1995 to 2001, academic and cultural exchanges dropped from 45,000 to 29,000 annually, and many accessible cultural centers and libraries were closed.[22] In 2003 the BBC World Service had 150 million weekly listeners around the globe while the VOA had fewer than 100 million.[23] Few Americans seemed to notice that with an information revolution occurring, soft power was becoming more rather than less important. Only after September 2001 did Americans rediscover the importance of investing in the instruments of soft power, and even then inadequately; in 2003 the Voice of America cut its English-language broadcasts by 25 percent.[24]

PUBLIC DIPLOMACY
IN THE INFORMATION AGE

Promoting positive images of one's country is not new, but the conditions for projecting soft power have been dramatically transformed in recent years. For one thing, nearly half the countries in the world are now democracies.[25] The Cold War model of a competition between two political and social systems has become less relevant as a guide for public diplomacy. While there is still a need to provide accurate information to populations in countries like Burma or Syria, where the government controls information, there is also a new need to create a favorable image in public opinion in countries like Mexico and Turkey, where parliaments can now affect decision making. When the United States sought support for the Iraq War in such countries, the administration's squandering of our soft power created a disabling rather than an enabling environment for its policies. Shaping public opinion becomes even more important where authoritarian governments have been replaced by new democracies. Even when foreign leaders are friendly, their leeway may be limited if their publics and parliaments have a negative image of the United States and its policies. In such circumstances, diplomacy aimed at public opinion can become as important to outcomes as the traditional classified diplomatic communications among leaders.

Information is power, and today a much larger part of the world's population has access to that power. Long gone are the days when "small teams of American foreign service officers drove Jeeps to the hinterlands of Latin America and other remote regions of the world to show reel-to-reel movies to isolated audiences."[26] Technological advances have led to a dramatic reduction in the cost of processing and transmitting information. The result is an explosion of information, one that has produced a "paradox of plenty."[27] Plenty of information leads to scarcity—of attention. When people are overwhelmed with the volume of information confronting them, they have difficulty discerning what to focus on. Attention rather than information becomes the scarce resource, and those who can distinguish valuable information from background clutter gain power. Editors and cue givers become more in demand, and this is a source of power for those who can tell us where to focus our attention.

In addition, publics have become more wary and sensitized about propaganda. Among editors and opinion leaders, credibility is the crucial resource, and an important source of soft power. Reputation becomes even more important than in the past, and political struggles occur over the creation and destruction of credibility. Governments compete for credibility not only with other governments, but with a broad range of alternatives including news media, corporations, nongovernmental organizations, intergovernmental organizations, and networks of scientific communities.

Politics has become a contest of competitive credibility. The world of traditional power politics is typically about whose military or economy wins. Politics in an information age "may ultimately be about whose story wins," say two RAND Corporation experts on politics and information.[28] Governments compete with each other and with other organizations to enhance their own credibility and weaken that of their opponents. Witness the struggle between Serbia and NATO to frame the interpretation of events in Kosovo in 1999 and the events in Serbia a year later. Prior to the demonstrations that led to the overthrow of Slobodan Milosevic in October 2000, 45 percent of Serb adults were tuned to Radio Free Europe and Voice of America, whereas only 31 percent listened to the state-controlled radio station, Radio Belgrade.[29] Moreover, Serbia's domestic alternative radio station, B92, provided access to Western news, and when the government tried to shut it down, it continued to provide such news on the Internet.[30]

Reputation has always mattered in world politics, but the role of credibility becomes an even more important power resource because of the "paradox of plenty." Information that appears to be propaganda may not only be scorned but also may turn out to be counterproductive if it undermines a country's reputation for credibility. Exaggerated claims about the imminence of Saddam Hussein's weapons of mass destruction and the strength of his ties to Al Qaeda may have helped mobilize domestic support for the Iraq War, but the subsequent disclosure of the exaggeration dealt a costly blow to British and American credibility. Under these new information age conditions of alternative sources of news, increasingly the soft sell may prove more effective than a hard sell.

THE SHAPE OF PUBLIC DIPLOMACY

In 1963, Edward R. Murrow, the noted broadcaster who was director of USIA in the Kennedy administration, defined public diplomacy as interactions aimed not only at foreign governments but primarily with nongovernmental individuals and organizations, and often presented as a variety of private views in addition to government views.[31] As Mark Leonard, a British expert on public diplomacy, has observed, skeptics who treat the term "public diplomacy" as a mere euphemism for propaganda miss the point. Simple propaganda often lacks credibility and thus is counterproductive as public diplomacy. Nor is public diplomacy merely public relations. Conveying information and selling a positive image is part of it, but public diplomacy also involves building long-term relationships that create an enabling environment for government policies.

There are three dimensions of public diplomacy; all three are important, and they require different relative proportions of direct government information and long-term cultural relationships.[32] The first and most immediate dimension is daily communications, which involves explaining the context of domestic and foreign policy decisions. After making decisions, government officials in modern democracies usually pay a good deal of attention to what to tell the press and how to do it. They generally focus on the domestic press—yet the foreign press corps has to be the most important target for the first dimension of public diplomacy. Leonard warns that many governments make the mistake of explaining domestic decisions only to their internal audiences and fail to realize the effect of their actions and the explanations of their actions on the international image of their country. For example, after a series of railroad accidents, the British press scornfully described Britain as "a third world country." Without explanation of the context, some of the foreign press repeated such phrases in their reporting, and that contributed to the image of Britain as a declining nation.

The day-to-day dimension must also involve preparation for dealing with crises and countering attacks. A rapid response capability means that false charges or misleading information can be answered immediately. For example, when Al Jazeera broadcast Osama bin Laden's first videotape on October 7, 2001, U.S. officials initially sought to prevent both Al Jazeera and American networks from broadcasting messages from bin Laden. But in the modern information age, that is not only as pointless as trying to stop the tide, but it also runs counter to the value of openness that America wants to symbolize. A better response would be to prepare to flood Al Jazeera and other networks with American voices to counter bin Laden's hate speech. While the Qatar-based broadcaster Al Jazeera and other foreign networks are hardly free of bias, they also need content. Indeed, their Washington bureau chief invited Americans, "Please come talk to us, exploit us."[33]

The second dimension is strategic communication, in which a set of simple themes is developed, much like what occurs in a political or advertising campaign. The campaign plans symbolic events and communications over the course of a year to brand the central themes, or to advance a particular government policy. Sometimes this is easier planned than done. For example, in the 1990s while the

British Council heavily promoted Britain as a modern, multiethnic, and creative island, another government agency, the British Tourist Authority, was busily advertising British tradition, ceremony, and history. Moreover, events can derail such branding. For example, several years of stressing the theme of Britain as a loyal member of the European Union were undone when, in 2003, Britain split with France and Germany to support the United States in the Iraq War. In the eyes of the public in many countries, this reinforced an undesirable image of Britain as America's servant.

Special themes focus on particular policy initiatives. For example, when the Reagan administration decided to implement NATO's decision to pursue a two-track policy of deploying missiles while negotiating to remove existing Soviet intermediate-range missiles, the Soviet Union responded with a concerted campaign to influence European opinion and make the deployment impossible. The United States themes stressed the multilateral nature of the NATO decision, encouraged European governments to take the lead when possible, and used nongovernmental American participants such as academic speakers effectively to counter Soviet arguments. Even though polls in Germany showed residual concerns about the policy, they also showed that two-thirds of the German public was pro-American. Former Secretary of State George Schultz later concluded, "I don't think we could have pulled it off if it hadn't been for a very active program of public diplomacy. Because the Soviets were very active all through 1983 . . . with peace movements and all kinds of efforts to dissuade our friends in Europe from deploying."[34]

The third dimension of public diplomacy is the development of lasting relationships with key individuals over many years through scholarships, exchanges, training, seminars, conferences, and access to media channels. Over the postwar decades, about 700,000 people have participated in American cultural and academic exchanges, and these exchanges have helped to educate world leaders like Anwar Sadat, Helmut Schmidt, and Margaret Thatcher.[35] Charlotte Beers, the former undersecretary of state for public diplomacy, has pointed out that such exchanges have involved over 200 current or former heads of state, and that half of the leaders in the coalition against terrorism were once exchange visitors. "This has got to be the best buy in government," she said.[36] Other countries have similar programs. For example, Japan has developed an interesting exchange program bringing 6,000 young foreigners each year from 40 countries to teach their languages in Japanese schools, with an alumni association to maintain the bonds of friendship that are developed.

Each of these three dimensions of public diplomacy plays an important role in helping to create an attractive image of a country and this can improve its prospects for obtaining its desired outcomes. But even the best advertising cannot sell an unpopular product, and, as we saw in chapter 2, policies that appear narrowly self-serving or are arrogantly presented are likely to consume rather than produce soft power. At best, long-standing friendly relationships may lead others to be slightly more tolerant in their responses. Sometimes friends will give you the benefit of the doubt or forgive more willingly.

A communications strategy cannot work if it cuts against the grain of policy. Actions speak louder than words, and public diplomacy that appears to be mere window dressing for the projection of hard power is unlikely to succeed. Sir Michael Butler, a British diplomat who admires the United States, explained, "If your government is perceived as self-interested, reactionary and unhelpful, it will seriously hamper your ability to get your way—as the U.S. is finding at the moment."[37] In 2003, Newt Gingrich, the former Speaker of the House of Representatives, attacked the State Department for failing to sell America's Iraq policy.[38] But selling requires paying attention to your markets, and on that dimension, the fault did not rest with the State Department. Gingrich also complained about the removal of the United States from the UN Human Rights Commission in 2001. But that was in retaliation for America's failure to pay its UN dues (a policy that originated in Congress) and the unilateral policies of the new Bush administration (which often originated in other executive departments, against the warnings of the State Department). Senator Charles Hagel, a Nebraska Republican, noted that after 9/11 many people in Washington were suddenly talking about the need for a renewed public diplomacy to "'get our message out.'. . . But Madison Avenue–style packaging cannot market a contradictory or confusing message. We need to reassess the fundamentals of our diplomatic approach. . . . Policy and diplomacy must match, or marketing becomes a confusing and transparent barrage of mixed messages."[39]

Effective public diplomacy is a two-way street that involves listening as well as talking. Soft power rests on some shared values. That is why exchanges are often more effective than mere broadcasting. By definition, soft power means getting others to want the same outcomes you want, and that requires understanding how they are hearing your messages, and fine-tuning it accordingly. It is crucial to understand the target audience. Yet research on foreign public opinion is woefully underfunded at about $5 million per year and has declined over the past decade.[40]

Preaching at foreigners is not the best way to convert them. Too often political leaders think that the problem is simply that others lack information, and that if they simply knew what we know, they would see things our way. But all information goes through cultural filters, and declamatory statements are rarely heard as intended. Telling is far less influential than actions and symbols that show as well as tell. That is why initiatives such as the Bush administration's push to increase development assistance or combat HIV/AIDS are so important.

Broadcasting is important but needs to be supplemented by effective "narrow casting"—targeting of messages for particular groups—via the Internet. Although the Internet reaches only the elites in the many parts of the world where most people are too poor to own a telephone, much less a computer, its flexibility and low cost allow for precise targeting. It also provides a way to transfer information to countries where the government blocks traditional media. And the Internet can be used interactively and in combination with exchanges. Face-to-face communications remain the most effective, but they can be supplemented and reinforced by the Internet. For example, a combination of visits and the Internet can create both virtual and real networks of young people who want to learn about each other's cultures. Or the United States might learn a lesson from Japan and pay young foreigners to spend a year teaching their language and culture in American schools. The alumni of these programs could then form associations that would remain connected over the Internet.

Some countries accomplish almost all of their public diplomacy through actions rather than broadcasting. Norway is a good example. It has only 5 million people, lacks an international language or transnational culture, is not a central location or hub of organizations or multinational corporate brands, and is not a member of the European Union. Nonetheless, as noted in chapter 1, it has developed a voice and presence out of proportion to its modest size and resources "through a ruthless prioritization of its target audiences and its concentration on a single message—Norway as a force for peace in the world."[41] The relevant activities include conflict mediation in the Middle East, Sri Lanka, and Colombia; the allocation of significant funds to foreign aid; and its frequent participation in peacekeeping forces. Of course, not all Norwegian actions are on message. The domestic politics of whaling sometimes strike a discordant note among environmentalists, but overall, Norway shows how a small country can exploit a diplomatic niche that enhances its image and role.

Not only do actions need to reinforce words, but also it is important to remember that the same words and images that are most successful in communicating to a domestic audience may have negative effects on a foreign audience. When President Bush used the term "axis of evil" to refer to Iraq, Iran, and North Korea in his 2002 State of the Union address, it was well received domestically, but foreigners reacted against his lumping together disparate diplomatic situations under a moralistic label. Similarly, while declaring a "war on terrorism" helped mobilize public and congressional support after 9/11, many foreign publics believed that the United States was making cooperation against terrorism more difficult, particularly when the idea of a war of indefinite duration could be used to incarcerate foreign prisoners.

Even when policy and communications are "in sync," wielding soft power resources in the information age is difficult. For one thing, as mentioned earlier, government communications are only a small fraction of the total communications among societies in an age that is awash in information. Hollywood movies that offend religious fundamentalists in other countries or activities by American missionaries that appear to devalue Islam will always be outside the control of government. Some skeptics have concluded that Americans should accept the inevitable, and let market forces take care of the presentation of their culture and image to foreigners. Why pour money into the Voice of America when CNN, MSNBC, or Fox can do the work for free? But such a conclusion is too facile. Market forces portray only the profitable mass dimensions of American culture, thus reinforcing foreign images of the United States as a one-dimensional country.

Government support of high-cultural exchanges has often had important effects on key foreign elites, as we saw in chapter 2. Developing long-term relationships is not always profitable in the short term, and thus leaving it simply to the market may lead to underinvestment. While higher education may pay for itself, and nonprofit organizations can help, many exchange programs would shrink without government support. Private companies must respond to market forces to stay in business. If there is no market for broadcasting in Serbo-Croatian or Pashtu, companies will not broadcast in those languages. And sometimes, private companies will cave in to political pressures from foreign governments if that boosts profits—witness the way Rupert Murdoch dropped the BBC, which broadcast some material critical of China, from his satellite television broadcasts to China in the 1990s.

At the same time, postmodern publics are generally skeptical of authority, and governments are often mistrusted. Thus it often behooves governments to keep in the background and to work with private actors. Some NGOs enjoy more trust than governments do, and though they are difficult to control, they can be useful channels of communication. American foundations such as the Ford Foundation, the Soros Foundation, and Carnegie Endowment and a variety of NGOs played an important role in the consolidation of democracy in Eastern Europe after the end of the Cold War. The Bill and Melinda Gates Foundation has done more than many governments to combat infectious diseases in Africa. For countries like Britain and the United States, which enjoy significant immigrant populations, diasporas can provide culturally sensitive and linguistically skilled connections. Building relationships between political parties in different countries was pioneered by Germany, where the major parties have foundations for building and maintaining foreign contacts that are partly supported by government funds. During the Reagan administration, the United States followed suit when it established the National Endowment for Democracy, which provided funds for the National Democratic Institute and the International Republican Institute as well as trade unions and chambers of commerce in order to promote democracy and civil society overseas.

American companies can also play an important role. Their representatives and brands directly touch the lives of far more people than government representatives do. Some public-spirited businesspeople have suggested that companies develop and provide sensitivity and communications training for corporate representatives before they are sent abroad. Companies can also take the lead in sponsoring specific public diplomacy projects such as "a technology company working with Sesame Workshops and a Lebanese broadcaster to co-produce an English language children's program centered on technology, an area of American achievement that is universally admired."[42]

Another benefit to indirect public diplomacy is that it is often able to take more risks in cultural exchanges. It is sometimes domestically difficult for the government to support cutting-edge art that appeals to foreign elites but offends popular tastes at home. For example, when the State Department mounted a show of modern art in 1947, it was ridiculed in the press for wasting taxpayer dollars, and even President Truman criticized it for showing the "vaporings of half-baked crazy people."[43] While governments are often loath to loosen their control by using indirect public diplomacy, what they lose in control they can more than make up in credibility by partnering with private organizations.

One way for a government to retain control while presenting the illusion of not doing so is by covert funding through intelligence agencies. For example, in the early stages of the Cold War, the Central Intelligence Agency covertly supported the budgets of cultural organizations such as the Congress for Cultural Freedom. Even at the time, there were misgivings. "In its starkest terms, the problem was how to use intellectual freedom as propaganda without turning it into propaganda in the process. . . . The political logic of this novel situation entailed the covert manipulation of liberal ideals and their proponents."[44] But secrecy works only so long as the secret can be kept, and that is difficult in the information age, particularly in a democracy like the United States with a powerful press, Congress, and no official secrets act, as Britain has. When disclosure eventually comes (as news of the CIA's involvement in cultural exchanges came through press reports and congressional hearings in the 1970s), the price in terms of lost credibility may be very high. It is generally better to be open about funding and establish an arms-length relationship.

This does not mean that the CIA plays no role in generating soft power. On the contrary, the development of trust and long-term relationships with friendly foreign intelligence agencies and the sharing of intelligence can have a powerful effect on other countries' perceptions of both the United States and world events. If soft power includes shaping others' perceptions, shared intelligence is an important soft-power resource. In such contexts, the sharing of classified information may have a direct and powerful effect on policy. Sometimes information alone, if telling and credible, can change another government's policy, which is why the intelligence failures and the exaggeration of intelligence for political ends in the prelude to the Iraq War were so damaging to American soft power. Not only was the general credibility of the government damaged, but a highly effective channel was also weakened. Other countries will be less likely to trust or believe American intelligence reports in the future.

The military can also play an important role in the creation of soft power. In addition to the aura of power that is generated by its hard-power capabilities, the military has a broad range of officer exchanges, joint-training, and assistance programs with other countries in peacetime. The Pentagon's international military and educational training programs include sessions on democracy and human rights along with military training. As former Secretary of Defense William Perry put it, such military-to-military contacts can constitute an aspect of "preventive defense," by developing contacts and helping to shape the outlook of foreign military officers more in line with American approaches. At various times, such contacts have provided channels of influence not available through ordinary diplomatic means. Indeed, some observers worry that America's five military regional commanders sometimes have more resources and better access in their regions than the American ambassadors in those countries.[45]

In wartime, military psychological operations ("psy-ops") are an important way to influence foreign behavior and even obviate outright military means. For example, an enemy outpost can be destroyed by a cruise missile or captured by ground forces—or enemy soldiers can be convinced to desert and leave the post undefended. Psy-ops often involve deception and disinformation that is effective in war but counterproductive in peace. Equally important in the tactics of war is the management of news to reduce unfavorable perceptions. Rigid censorship is not always the answer. An aspect of soft power that the Pentagon got right in the second Gulf War has been called the "weaponization of reporters." Embedding reporters with forward military units limited Saddam Hussein's ability to create international outrage by claiming that Americans were deliberately killing civilians. Unlike the first Gulf War, when CNN framed the issues, the diffusion of information technology and the rise of new outlets like Al Jazeera in the ensuing decade required a new strategy for avoiding damage to American soft power in the context of war. Whatever other issues it raised, embedding reporters in front-line units was a successful tactic under wartime conditions in the information age.

The problems with the military role in wielding soft power arise when it tries to apply wartime tactics in ambiguous situations. This is particularly tempting in the current ill-defined war on terrorism, which blurs the distinction between normal civilian activities and war. In 2002, frustrated with American public diplomacy, the Pentagon developed plans for the Office of Strategic Influence, which would provide news items, possibly including false ones, to foreign media organizations in an effort to influence both friendly and unfriendly countries.[46] After the plans were revealed in the press, Secretary of Defense Rumsfeld had to quickly disavow the project. But the damage to American credibility and soft power had already been done.

Finally, it is a mistake to see public diplomacy simply in adversarial terms. Sometimes there is a competition of "my information versus your information," but often there can be gains for both sides. German public diplomacy during the Cold War is a good example. In contrast to French public diplomacy, which sought to demonstrate independence from the United States, a key theme of German public diplomacy was to portray itself as a reliable ally in American eyes. Thus German and American policy information goals were mutually reinforcing.[47] Political leaders may share mutual and similar objectives—for example the promotion of democracy and human rights. In such circumstances, there can be joint gains from coordination of public diplomacy programs. Cooperative public diplomacy can also help take the edge off suspicions of narrow national motives.[48]

In addition, there are times when cooperation, including the enhancement of the public image of multilateral institutions like NATO or the UN, can make it easier for governments to use such instruments to handle difficult tasks like peacekeeping, promoting democracy, or countering terrorism. For example, during the Cold

War, American public diplomacy in Czechoslovakia was reinforced by the association of the United States with international conventions that fostered human rights.[49] In 1975, the multilateral Helsinki Conference on Security and Cooperation in Europe (CSCE) legitimized discussion of human rights behind the Iron Curtain and had consequences that were unforeseen by those who signed the agreement that resulted, called the Final Act. As former CIA director Robert Gates concluded, despite initial American resistance, "The Soviets desperately wanted the CSCE, they got it, and it laid the foundations for the end of their empire."[50]

THE SPECIAL CASE OF THE MIDDLE EAST

The Middle East presents a particular challenge for American soft power and public diplomacy. Not only was it the home of the terrorists who attacked the United States on September 11, 2001, but the region has not adjusted well to modernization. Half the world's countries are democracies, yet none of the 22 Arab countries is democratic. Economic growth has been slow, approximately half the women are illiterate, and the region is not well integrated with the world economy. In 2003, the World Bank reported that annual income growth per head in the region averaged a mere .5 percent from 1985 to 2000, while military spending was the highest in the world at 6 percent of GDP.[51] With a population over 300 million, the Arab countries export less to the world, excluding oil and gas, than does Finland.[52] The number of scientists working in Arab countries is about one-third of the global average.[53] There is an enormous "youth bulge" in the demographic tables, yet the region has inadequate opportunities for young people to find meaningful work. Forty-five percent of the population of the Arab world is now under the age of 14, and the population as a whole will double over the next quarter century. Unemployment hovers at 20 percent.[54] At the same time, the Middle East is awash with modern communications, much of it with an anti-American slant. As we saw from the figures in chapter 2, this region presents a special challenge for public diplomacy.

During the Cold War, the United States' approach to the region was to foster stability, which would prevent the spread of Soviet influence, ensure the supply of oil for the world economy, and provide security for Israel, one of the rare democracies. The American strategy was management through autocratic leaders, and "Don't rock the boat." During the Reagan administration, the United States even supported Saddam Hussein as a counterbalance to the Islamic regime that had overthrown America's ally, the shah of Iran. According to Edward Walker, the president of the Middle East Institute who has served as ambassador to several countries in the region, "While we spoke of human rights, economic development, democracy and the rule of law, our policies and the distribution of our resources did not reflect our rhetoric. We neither challenged the governments in the region to change nor offered incentives to help stimulate change."[55]

After 9/11, the Bush administration launched an ambitious new approach. Drawing on the analogy of the Cold War and the American role in the transformation of Europe, the administration decided that the United States should commit to a long-term transformation of the Middle East. The removal of Saddam Hussein was only a first step. National Security Adviser Condoleezza Rice argued that "much as a democratic Germany became a linchpin of a new Europe that is today whole, free and at peace, so a transformed Iraq can become a key element in a very different Middle East in which the ideologies of hate will not flourish."[56] But the exercise of hard power in the four-week campaign that toppled Saddam Hussein was the easy part. Germany (and Japan) were postwar success stories, but both were relatively homogeneous societies with significant middle classes and no organized resistance to American occupation. Moreover, Iraq's possession of oil is a mixed blessing, since few oil-based economies have proved hospitable for liberal democracy. And, as we saw in chapter 2, democratization after World War II took years and was greatly assisted by American soft power. The long-run strategy for the transformation of Iraq and the Middle East will not succeed without a similar role for American (and others') soft power.

The Cold War analogy is useful in suggesting the need for a long-term strategy, but it can also mislead. Soft power depends on willing receivers, and the cultural differences between the United States and Europe were not as great as those between the United States and the Middle East. Thus Europe was more susceptible to American soft-power resources. On the other hand, cultural differences did not prevent democracy from taking root in Japan or South Korea, albeit with a four-decade lag in the latter case. And democracy works in other Muslim countries such as Turkey and Bangladesh. The cultural barriers are far from insurmountable.

Democracy is more than mere voting, which can lead to "one man, one vote, once" if done too hastily. Since the autocratic regimes in the Middle East have destroyed their liberal opposition, radical Islamists often represent the only alternative dissent in many countries. The radical Islamists feed on resistance to corrupt regimes, opposition to American policies, and popular fears of modernization. They portray liberal democracy as represented by corruption, sex, and violence, and American films and television sometimes reinforce that portrait. At the same time, modernization also produces education, jobs, more opportunities, and better health care. Fortunately, polls show that the majority of the populations in the region desire the benefits of trade, communications, and globalization. As we saw in chapter 2, American technology is widely admired. Given this ambivalence among the moderates in the Arab cultures, there is still a chance of isolating the extremists.

Democracy cannot be imposed by force. The key to success will lie in policies that open regional economies, reduce bureaucratic controls, speed economic growth, improve educational systems, and encourage the types of gradual political changes that are taking place in small countries like Bahrain, Oman, Kuwait, and Morocco. The development of intellectuals, social groups, and eventually countries that demonstrate that liberal democracy can be consistent with local cultures could have beneficial effects similar to the ways that Japan and Korea demonstrated that democracy can be combined with indigenous values in Asia. But that takes time, as well as skillful application of American soft-power resources.

Soon after 9/11, many Americans were transfixed by the question "Why do they hate us?" But the answer was that many Arabs feared, misunderstood, and opposed American policies, but nonetheless admired some aspects of American culture. Moreover, they share many values such as family, religious belief, and desire for democracy. The grounds for soft power exist, but the world's leading communications country has proved surprisingly maladroit in exploiting those opportunities. For example, a major effort to produce television advertisements that showed American Muslims being well treated at home had little effect. According to critics, the ground had not been well prepared by polls and focus groups, and many people in the region were more concerned with what they saw as the deficiencies of American policies rather than American domestic conditions. The problematic result has been "a public diplomacy that accentuates image over substance."[57] As Danielle Pletka of the American Enterprise Institute put it, "We are seen as propping up these lousy governments. No amount of Britney Spears will counter the anti-Western teachings that many youths in closed societies grow up with."[58]

In 2003, a bipartisan advisory group on public diplomacy for the Arab and Muslim world found that the United States was spending only $150 million on public diplomacy in Muslim-majority countries, including $25 million on outreach programs. They concluded, "To say that financial resources are inadequate to the task is a gross understatement."[59] In addition to the appointment of a new White House director of public diplomacy, they recommended building libraries and information centers, translating more Western books into Arabic, increasing scholarships and visiting fellowships, upgrading the American Internet presence, and training more Arabic speakers and public relations specialists.

Like all public diplomacy, effective public diplomacy in the region will have three dimensions. The United States will have to become more agile in the first dimension, quick response and explanation of current events. New broadcasting units like Radio Sawa, which broadcasts in Arabic and intersperses news with popular music, is a step in the right direction, but the Americans will also have to work more effectively with local media such as Al Jazeera and Al Arabiya. The second dimension, development of a few strategic themes, will have to include better explanations of American policies in addition to branding America as a democratic nation. For example, the charge that American policies are indifferent to the destruction of Muslim lives can be addressed head-on by pointing to American interventions that saved Muslim lives in Bosnia and Kosovo, as well as assistance to Muslim countries to foster development and combat AIDS. As Assistant Secretary of State for Near Eastern Affairs William Burns has pointed out, democratic change must be embedded in "a wider positive agenda for the region, alongside rebuilding Iraq, achieving the President's two-state vision for Israelis and Palestinians; and modernizing Arab economies."[60]

Most important, however, will be the development of a long-term strategy of cultural and educational exchanges that develop a richer and more open civil society in Middle Eastern countries. The most effective spokesmen for the United States are not Americans but indigenous surrogates who understand America's virtues as well as our faults. A fascinating example of this is taking place right now between Los Angeles and Teheran as the Iranian diaspora has been broadcasting a privately sponsored television program into Iran to encourage reform in that country.[61]

Much of the work of developing an open civil society can be promoted by corporations, foundations, universities, and other non-profit organizations, as well as by governments. Companies and foundations can offer technology to help modernize Arab educational systems and take them beyond rote learning. American universities can establish more exchange programs for students and faculty. Foundations can support the development of institutions of American studies in Arab countries, or programs that enhance the professionalism of journalists. Governments can support the teaching of the English language and finance student exchanges. In short, there are many strands to an effective long-term strategy for creating soft-power resources and promoting conditions for the development of democracy. But, as I argued earlier, none will be effective unless the style and substance of American policies are consistent with the larger democratic message.

THE FUTURE OF
AMERICAN PUBLIC DIPLOMACY

Americans rediscovered the need for public diplomacy after September 11, but we have still not adjusted to the complexities of wielding soft power in the global information age. Some people now regard the abolition of USIA as a mistake, but there is no consensus about recreating it as opposed to reorganizing its functions, which were dispersed within the State Department.[62] The Broadcasting Board of Governors oversees the Voice of America as well as a number of specialized stations that focus on particular countries. A number of useful steps have been taken, such as the establishment of Radio Sawa and Radio Farda, which broadcasts to Iran. An Office of Global Communication has been created in the White House. But much more is needed.

Perhaps most striking is the low priority and paucity of resources devoted to producing soft power. The combined cost of the State Department's public diplomacy programs and U.S. international broadcasting comes to a little over a billion dollars, about 4 percent of the nation's international affairs budget, about 3 percent of the intelligence budget, and .29 percent of the military budget. If we spent 1 percent of the military budget on public diplomacy—or, as Newton Minow, the former chair of the FCC, would say, "one dollar to launch ideas for every one hundred dollars we invest to launch bombs"—it would mean almost a quadrupling of the existing budget.[63] The United States still invests far less in soft-power resources than do other major countries, as shown in Table 4.1.

Table 4.1 Comparative Investments in Soft and Hard Power

	Public Diplomacy	Defense	Year
United States	$1.12B	$347.9B	2002
France	$1.05B	$33.6B	2001
Great Britain	$1.00B	$38.4B	2002
Germany	$218M	$27.5B	2001
Japan	$210M	$40.3B	2001

Equally important is to establish more policy coherence among the dimensions of public diplomacy and to relate them to other issues. For example, despite a declining share of the market for international students, "The U.S. government seems to lack overall strategic sense of why exchange is important. . . . In this strategic vacuum, it is difficult to counter the day-to-day obstacles that students encounter in trying to come here."[64] There is little coordination of exchange policy with visa policies. After 9/11, Americans became more fearful. As one observer noted, "While greater vigilance is certainly needed, this broad net is catching all kinds of people who are no danger whatsoever."[65] By needlessly discouraging people from coming to the United States who could make a valuable contribution to international understanding, such policies undercut our soft-power resources.

Public diplomacy needs greater support in the White House. A task force on public diplomacy of the Council on Foreign Relations has urged the creation of an office to be called the Public Diplomacy Coordinating Structure in the White House, to be led by a presidential designee. In addition, new institutions could be created to help mobilize the private sector. This could also be accomplished by creating a nonprofit entity to be called the Corporation for Public Diplomacy to organize private sector efforts.[66] A successful strategy would need to focus not merely on broadcasting American messages but on two-way communications that engage more of the nongovernmental dimensions of society.

Above all, however, Americans will have to become more aware of cultural differences. To be effective, we must become less parochial and more sensitive to foreign perceptions. President Bush's comments at a White House press conference on October 11, 2001, illustrate the nature of our problem: "I am amazed that there is such a misunderstanding of what our country is about that people would hate us. . . . Like most Americans, I just can't believe it. Because I know how good we are, and we've got to do a better job of making our case." But the first step in making a better case is a greater understanding of how our policies appear to others and of the cultural filters that affect how they hear our messages.

American media coverage of the rest of the world declined dramatically after the end of the Cold War. Training in foreign languages lags. When we become irritated with French policy on Iraq, Congressmen rename "French fries" as "freedom fries." Fewer scholars take up Fulbright visiting lectureships. One historian noted "how distant we are from a time when American historians—driven by a curiosity about the world beyond both the academy and the United States—were able to communicate with the public about the issues, national and international, that continue to affect us all."[67] To be more effective in public diplomacy in the global information age, we need to change attitudes at home as well as abroad. To put it bluntly, to communicate more effectively, Americans need to listen. Wielding soft power is far less unilateral than employing hard power, and we have yet to learn that lesson.

Soft Power and
American Foreign Policy

ANTI-AMERICANISM HAS INCREASED in the past few years. Thomas Pickering, a seasoned diplomat, considered 2003 "as high a zenith of anti-Americanism as we've seen for a long time."[1] Polls show that our soft-power losses can be traced largely to our foreign policy. "A widespread and fashionable view is that the United States is a classically imperialist power. . . . That mood has been expressed in different ways by different people, from the hockey fans in Montreal who boo the American national anthem to the high school students in Switzerland who do not want to go to the United States as exchange students."[2] An Australian observer concluded that "the lesson of Iraq is that the US's soft power is in decline. Bush went to war having failed to win a broader military coalition or UN authorization. This had two direct consequences: a rise in anti-American sentiment, lifting terrorist recruitment; and a higher cost to the US for the war and reconstruction effort."[3] Pluralities in 15 out of 24 countries responding to a Gallup International poll said that American foreign policies had a negative effect on their attitudes toward the United States.

A Eurobarometer poll found that a majority of Europeans believe that the United States tends to play a negative role in fighting global poverty, protecting the environment, and maintaining peace in the world.[4] When asked in a Pew poll to what extent they thought the United States "takes your interests into account," a majority in 20 out of 42 countries surveyed said "Not too much" or "Not at all."[5] In many countries, unfavorable ratings were highest among younger people. American pop culture may be widely admired among young people, but the unpopularity of our foreign policies is making the next generation question American power.[6]

American music and films are more popular in Britain, France, and Germany than they were 20 years ago, another period when American policies were unpopular in Europe, but the attraction of our policies is even lower than it was then.[7] There are also hints that unpopular foreign policies might be spilling over and undercutting the attractiveness of some other aspects of American popular culture. A 2003 Roper study showed that "for the first time since 1998, consumers in 30 countries signaled their disenchantment with America by being less likely to buy Nike products or eat at McDonald's. . . . At the same time, 9 of the top 12 Asian and European firms, including Sony, BMW and Panasonic, saw their scores rise."[8]

THE COSTS OF IGNORING SOFT POWER

Skeptics about soft power say not to worry. Popularity is ephemeral and should not be a guide for foreign policy in any case. The United States can act without the world's applause. We are so strong we can do as we wish. We are the world's only superpower, and that fact is bound to engender envy and resentment. Fouad Ajami has stated recently, "The United States need not worry about hearts and minds in foreign lands."[9] Columnist Cal Thomas refers to "the fiction that our enemies can be made less threatening by what America says and does."[10] Moreover, the United States has been unpopular in the past yet managed to recover. We do not need permanent allies and institutions. We can always pick up a coalition of the willing when we need to. Donald Rumsfeld is wont to say that the issues should determine the coalitions, not vice versa.

But it would be a mistake to dismiss the recent decline in our attractiveness so lightly. It is true that the United States has recovered from unpopular policies in the past, but that was against the backdrop of the Cold War, in which other countries still feared the Soviet Union as the greater evil. Moreover, as we saw in chapter 2, while the United States' size and association with disruptive modernity is real and unavoidable, smart policies can soften the sharp edges of that reality and reduce the resentments they engender. That is what the U.S. did after World War II. We used our soft-power resources and co-opted others into a set of alliances and institutions that lasted for 60 years. We won the Cold War against the Soviet Union with a strategy of containment that used our soft power as well as our hard power.

It is true that the new threat of transnational terrorism increased American vulnerability, and some of our unilateralism after September 11 was driven by fear. But the United States cannot meet the new threat identified in the national security strategy without the cooperation of other countries. They will cooperate up to a point out of mere self-interest, but their degree of cooperation is also affected by the attractiveness of the United States. Take Pakistan for example. President Pervez Musharraf faces a complex game of cooperating with the United States in the war on terrorism while managing a large anti-American constituency at home. He winds up balancing concessions and retractions. If the United States were more attractive to the Pakistani populace, we would see more concessions in the mix.

It is not smart to discount soft power as just a question of image, public relations, and ephemeral popularity. As we argued earlier, it is a form of power—a means of obtaining desired outcomes. When we discount the importance of our attractiveness to other countries, we pay a price. Most important, if the United States is so unpopular in a country that being pro-American is a kiss of death in that country's domestic politics, political leaders are unlikely to make concessions to help us. Turkey, Mexico, and Chile were prime examples in the run-up to the Iraq War in March 2003. When American policies lose their legitimacy and credibility in the eyes of others, attitudes of distrust tend to fester and further reduce our leverage. For example, after 9/11 there was an outpouring of sympathy from Germans for the United States, and Germany joined a military campaign against the Al Qaeda network. But as the United States geared up for the unpopular Iraq War, Germans expressed widespread disbelief about the reasons the U.S. gave for going to war such as the alleged connection of Iraq to 9/11 and the imminence of the threat of weapons of mass destruction. German suspicions were reinforced by what they saw as biased American media coverage during the war, and by the failure to find weapons of mass destruction or prove the connection to 9/11 in the aftermath of the war. The combination fostered a climate in which conspiracy theories flourished. By July 2003, according to a Reuters poll, one-third of Germans under the age of 30 said that they thought the American government might even have staged the original September 11 attacks.[11]

Absurd views feed upon each other, and paranoia can be contagious. American attitudes toward foreigners harden, and we begin to believe that the rest of the world really does hate us. Some Americans begin to hold grudges, to mistrust all Muslims, to boycott French wines and rename French fries, to spread and believe false rumors.[12] In turn, foreigners see Americans as uninformed and insensitive to anyone's interests but their own. They see our media wrapped in the American flag. Some Americans in turn succumb to residual strands of isolationism, and say that if others choose to see us that way, "To hell with 'em." If foreigners are going to be like that, who cares whether we are popular or not. But to the extent that Americans allow ourselves to become isolated, we embolden our enemies such as Al Qaeda. Such reactions undercut our soft power and are self-defeating in terms of the outcomes we want.

Some hard-line skeptics might say that whatever the merits of soft power, it has little role to play in the current war on terrorism. Osama bin Laden and his followers are repelled, not attracted, by American culture, values, and policies. Military power was essential in defeating the Taliban government in Afghanistan, and soft power will never convert fanatics. Charles Krauthammer, for example, argued soon after our swift military victory in Afghanistan that it proved that "the new unilateralism" worked. That is true up to a point, but the skeptics mistake half the answer for the whole solution.

Look again at Afghanistan. Precision bombing and Special Forces defeated the Taliban government, but U.S. forces in Afghanistan wrapped up less than a quarter of Al Qaeda, a transnational network with cells in 60 countries. The United States cannot bomb Al Qaeda cells in Hamburg, Kuala Lumpur, or Detroit. Success against them depends on close civilian cooperation, whether sharing intelligence, coordinating police work across borders, or tracing global financial flows. America's partners work with us partly out of self-interest, but the inherent attractiveness of U.S. policies can and does influence their degree of cooperation.

Equally important, the current struggle against Islamist terrorism is not a clash of civilizations but a contest whose outcome is closely tied to a civil war between moderates and extremists within Islamic civilization. The United States and other advanced democracies will win only if moderate Muslims win, and the ability to attract the moderates is critical to victory. We need to adopt policies that appeal to moderates, and to use public diplomacy more effectively to explain our common interests. We need a better strategy for wielding our soft power. We will have to learn better to combine hard and soft power if we wish to meet the new challenges.

As we saw in chapter 1, beneath the surface structure, the world changed in profound ways during the last decades of the twentieth century. September 11 was like a flash of lightning on a summer evening that displayed an altered landscape, and we are still left groping in the dark wondering how to find our way through it. George W. Bush entered office committed to a traditional realist foreign policy that would focus on great powers like China and Russia, and eschew nation building in failed states of the less developed world. But in September 2002, his administration proclaimed a new national security strategy that was based on the recognition that, as Bush said, "We are menaced less by fleets and armies than by catastrophic technologies falling into the hands of the embittered few." Instead of engaging in strategic rivalry, Bush declared, "Today, the world's great powers find ourselves on the same side—united by common dangers of terrorist violence and chaos." The United States increased its development assistance and its efforts to combat AIDS because "weak states, like Afghanistan, can pose as great a danger to our national interest as strong states."[13] The historian John Lewis Gaddis compared the new strategy to the seminal days that redefined American foreign policy in the 1940s after World War II.[14]

The new strategy attracted criticism at home and abroad for its excessive rhetoric about preemptive military strikes and the promotion of American primacy. Critics pointed out that the practice of preemption is not new, but turning it into a doctrine weakens international norms and encourages other countries to engage in risky actions. Similarly, American primacy is a fact, but there was no need for rhetoric that rubs other peoples' noses in it. Notwithstanding such flaws, the new strategy was a response to the deep trends in world politics that were illuminated by the events of September 11, 2001. The "privatization of war"—by, for example, transnational groups such as Al Qaeda—is a major historical change in world politics that must be addressed. This is what the new Bush strategy gets right. What the United States has not yet sorted out is how to go about implementing the new approach. We have done far better on identifying the ends than the means. On that dimension, both the administration and the Congress were deeply divided.

According to the national security strategy, the greatest threats that the American people face are transnational terrorism and weapons of mass destruction, and particularly their combination. Yet meeting the challenge posed by transnational military organizations that could acquire weapons of mass destruction requires the cooperation of other countries—and cooperation is strengthened by soft power. Similarly, efforts to promote democracy in Iraq and elsewhere will require the help of others. Reconstruction in Iraq and peacekeeping in failed states are far more likely to succeed and to be less costly if shared with others rather than appearing to be American imperial occupation. The fact that the United States squandered its soft power in the way that it went to war meant that the aftermath turned out to be much more costly than it need have been.

Even after the war, in the hubris and glow of victory in May 2003, the United States resisted giving a significant international role to the United Nations and others in Iraq. But as casualties and costs mounted over the summer, the U.S. found many other countries reluctant to share the burden without a UN blessing. As the top American commander for Iraq, General John Abizaid, reported, "You can't underestimate the public perception both within Iraq and within the Arab world about the percentage of the force being so heavily American." But, Abizaid continued, other countries "need to have their internal political constituents satisfied that they're playing a role as an instrument of the international community and not as a pawn of the United States." Before the Madrid conference of potential donors to Iraq in October 2003, the *New York Times* reported that L. Paul Bremer, the chief occupation administrator in Baghdad, said, "I need the money so bad we have to move off our principled opposition to the international community being in charge."[15] Neoconservative commentators such as Max Boot urged conservatives not to treat marginalizing the UN as a core principle, and Charles Krauthammer, proud author of "the new unilateralism," called for a new UN resolution because, he said, Russia, India, and others "say they would contribute only under such a resolution. . . . The U.S. is not overstretched. But psychologically we are up against our limits. The American people are simply not prepared to undertake worldwide nation building."[16]

In the global information age, the attractiveness of the United States will be crucial to our ability to achieve the outcomes we want. Rather than having to put together pickup coalitions of the willing for each new game, we will benefit if we are able to attract others into institutional alliances and eschew weakening those we have already created. NATO, for example, not only aggregates the capabilities of advanced nations, but its interminable committees, procedures, and exercises also allow them to train together and quickly become interoperable when a crisis occurs. As for alliances, if the United States is an attractive source of security and reassurance, other countries will set their expectations in directions that are conducive to our interests. For example, initially the U.S.-Japan security treaty, signed in 1951, was not very popular in Japan, but over the decades, polls show that it became more attractive to the Japanese public. Once that happened, Japanese politicians began to build it into their approaches to foreign policy. The United States benefits when it is regarded as a constant and trusted source of attraction, so that other countries are not obliged continually to reexamine their options in an atmosphere of uncertain coalitions. In the Japan case, broad acceptance of the U.S. by the Japanese public "contributed to the maintenance of US hegemony" and "served as political constraints compelling the ruling elites to continue cooperation with the United States."[17] Popularity can contribute to stability.

Finally, as the RAND Corporation's John Arquilla and David Ronfeldt argue, power in the global information age will come not just from strong defenses, but from strong sharing. A traditional realpolitik mind-set makes it difficult to share with others. But in the information age, such sharing not only enhances the ability of others to cooperate with us but also increases their inclination to do so.[18] As we share intelligence and capabilities with others, we develop common outlooks and approaches that improve our ability to deal with the new challenges. Power flows from that attraction. Dismissing the importance of attraction as merely ephemeral popularity ignores key insights from new theories of leadership as well as the new realities of the information age. We cannot afford that.

AMERICAN EMPIRE?

Not everyone agrees with this picture of the changing nature of world politics, and thus they recommend a different approach to American foreign policy. Many argue that our new vulnerability requires a much higher degree of forceful control. Moreover, our unprecedented power now makes it possible. The writer Robert Kaplan has argued, "It is a cliché these days to observe that the United States now possesses a global empire; the question now is how the American empire should operate on a tactical level to manage an unruly world."[19] William Kristol, editor of the neoconservative magazine *The Weekly Standard*, says, "We need to err on the side of being strong. And if people want to say we're an imperialist power, fine."[20] Writing in the same journal in 2001, Max Boot agreed in the explicitly titled article "The Case for an American Empire."[21]

Three decades ago, the radical Left used the term "American empire" as a disparaging epithet. Now the phrase has come out of the closet and is used by a number of analysts on both the Left and the Right to explain and guide American foreign policy. Andrew Bacevich, for example, argues that the notion of an American empire is approaching mainstream respectability, and we should not worry about the semantic details—the negative connotations of the word "empire."[22] But words matter. In *Alice in Wonderland*, the Red Queen tells Alice that she can make words mean whatever she wants. But the world of the twenty-first century is not Wonderland. If we want to communicate clearly with others, we have to take care what we use our words to do. If America is like no other empire in history, as Bacevich claims, then in what sense is it an empire? The use of the term may point up some useful analogies, but it may also mislead us and others by obscuring important differences.

In many ways the metaphor of empire is seductive. The American military has a global reach with bases around the world and its regional commanders sometimes act like proconsuls and are even called proconsuls in the press. English is a lingua franca like Latin. The American economy is the largest in the world, and American culture serves as a magnet. But it is a mistake to confuse the politics of primacy with the politics of empire. Though unequal relationships certainly exist between the United States and weaker powers, and can be conducive to exploitation, absent formal political control, the term "imperial" can be misleading. Its acceptance would be a disastrous guide for American foreign policy because it fails to take into account how the world has changed. The United States is certainly not an empire in the way we think of the European overseas empires of the nineteenth and twentieth centuries because the core feature of such imperialism was direct political control.[23] The United States has more power resources than Britain had at its imperial peak. On the other hand, the U.S. has less control over the behavior that occurs inside other countries than Britain did when it ruled a quarter of the globe. For example, Kenya's schools, taxes, laws and elections—not to mention external relations—were controlled by British officials. Even where Britain used indirect rule through local potentates, as in Uganda, it exercised far more control than the United States does today. Some try to rescue the metaphor by referring to "informal empire" or the "imperialism of free trade," but this simply obscures important differences in degrees of control suggested by comparisons with real historical empires. Yes, the Americans have widespread influence, but in 2003, the United States could not even get Mexico and Chile to vote for a second resolution on Iraq in the UN Security Council. The British Empire did not have that kind of problem with Kenya or India.

Devotees of the new imperialism say, "Don't be so literal. 'Empire' is merely a metaphor." But the problem with the metaphor is it implies a control from Washington that is unrealistic, and reinforces the prevailing strong temptations toward unilateralism that are present in Congress and parts of the administration. As we saw in chapter 1, the costs of occupation of other countries has become prohibitive in a world of multiple nationalisms, and the legitimacy of empire is broadly challenged.

We also saw that power depends on context, and the distribution of power differs greatly in different domains. We saw that in the global information age, power is distributed among countries in a pattern that resembles a complex three-dimensional chess game. On the top chessboard of political-military issues, military power is largely unipolar, but on the economic board, in the middle, the

United States is not a hegemon or an empire, and it must bargain as an equal when Europe acts in a unified way. And on the bottom chessboard of transnational relations, power is chaotically dispersed, and it makes no sense to use traditional terms such as "unipolarity," "hegemony," or "American empire." Those who recommend an imperial American foreign policy based on traditional military descriptions of American power are relying on a woefully inadequate analysis. If you are in a three-dimensional game, you will lose if you focus only on one board and fail to notice the other boards and the vertical connections among them—witness the connections in the war on terrorism between military actions on the top board, where we removed a dangerous tyrant in Iraq, but simultaneously increased the ability of the Al Qaeda network to gain new recruits on the bottom, transnational, board.[24]

Because of its leading edge in the information revolution and its past investment in military power, the United States will likely remain the world's single most powerful country well into the twenty-first century. French dreams of a multipolar military world are unlikely to be realized anytime soon, and the German foreign minister, Joschka Fischer, has explicitly eschewed such a goal.[25] But not all the important types of power come out of the barrel of a gun. Hard power is relevant to getting the outcomes we want on all three chessboards, but many of the transnational issues such as climate change, the spread of infectious diseases, international crime, and terrorism cannot be resolved by military force alone. Representing the dark side of globalization, these issues are inherently multilateral and require cooperation for their solution. Soft power is particularly important in dealing with the issues that arise from the bottom chessboard, transnational relations. To describe such a three-dimensional world as an American empire fails to capture the real nature of the foreign policy tasks that we face.

Another problem for those who urge that we accept the idea of an American empire is that they misunderstand the underlying nature of American public opinion and institutions. Even if it is true that unilateral occupation and transformation of undemocratic regimes in the Middle East and elsewhere would reduce some of the sources of transnational terrorism, the question is whether the American public will tolerate an imperial role for its government. Neoconservative writers such as Max Boot argue that the United States should provide troubled countries with the sort of enlightened foreign administration once provided by self-confident Englishmen in jodphurs and pith helmets, but, as the British historian Niall Ferguson points out, modern America differs from nineteenth-century Britain in our "chronically short time frame."[26] Although an advocate of empire, Ferguson worries that the American political system is not up to the task, and, for better or for worse, he is right.

The United States has intervened and governed countries in Central America, the Caribbean, and the Philippines, and was briefly tempted into real imperialism when it emerged as a world power a century ago, but the formal imperial interlude did not last.[27] Unlike for the British, for Americans imperialism has never been a comfortable experience, and only a small portion of the cases of American military occupation led directly to the establishment of democracies. The establishment of democracy in Germany and Japan after World War II remains the exception rather than the rule, and in these countries it took nearly a decade. American empire is not limited by "imperial overstretch" in the sense of costing an impossible portion of our GDP. We devoted a much higher percentage of GDP to the military budget during the Cold War than we do today. The overstretch will come from having to police more and more peripheral countries with nationally resistant publics than foreign or American public opinion will accept. Polls show little taste for empire among Americans. Instead, the American public continues to say that it favors multilateralism and working with the UN. Perhaps that is why Michael Ignatieff, a Canadian advocate of accepting the empire metaphor, qualifies it by referring to the American role in the world as "Empire Lite."[28]

In fact, the problem of creating an American empire might better be termed "imperial understretch." Neither the public nor Congress has proved willing to invest seriously in the instruments of nation building and governance as opposed to military force. The entire budget for the State Department (including AID, the Agency for International Development) is only 1 percent of the federal budget. The United States spends nearly 17 times as much on its military as it does on foreign affairs, and there is little indication that this is about to change in an era of tax cuts and budget deficits. Moreover, our military is designed for fighting rather than police work, and the Pentagon under Secretary of Defense Donald Rumsfeld initially cut back on training for peacekeeping operations. The U.S. has designed a military that is better suited to kick down the door, beat up a dictator, and then go home rather than stay for the harder imperial work of building a democratic polity. For a variety of reasons, both about the world and about the United States, Americans should avoid the misleading metaphor of empire as a guide for our foreign policy. Empire is not the narrative we need to help us understand and cope with the global information age of the twenty-first century.

AMERICAN FOREIGN POLICY TRADITIONS

As we saw in chapter 2, the United States has a variety of foreign policy traditions to draw on that overlap, reinforce, and sometimes conflict with each other. The writer Walter Mead has used the device of identifying these traditions with the names of past leaders as a helpful way to distinguish them.[29] The realists, who prudently pursue national interest and commerce, are named after Alexander Hamilton. Populists, who emphasize self-reliance and frequent use of coercion, he names for Andrew Jackson. He calls "Jeffersonians" those who advocate the pursuit of democracy by being a shining beacon to others rather than (in John Quincy Adams's words) "going forth in search of dragons to destroy." Finally, "Wilsonians" are the idealists who follow Woodrow Wilson in seeking to make the world safe for democracy.

Each approach has its virtues and faults. The Hamiltonians are prudent, but their realism lacks a moral appeal to many at home and abroad. The Jacksonians are robust and tough, but lack staying power and allies. Both the Hamiltonians and Jacksonians fail to accord adequate importance to soft power. The Jeffersonians, on the other hand, have plenty of soft power, but not enough hard power. As we saw in chapter 1, being a shining city on a hill is attractive but often is not sufficient to achieve all foreign policy goals. The Wilsonians are also long on soft power, but sometimes their idealism leads them to develop unrealistic ambitions. Their danger is that their foreign policy vehicles often have strong accelerators but weak brakes and are thus prone to go off the road.

Whereas Hamiltonians and Jeffersonians tend toward prudent and conservative foreign policies that do not rock the boat, Wilsonians seek to transform the international situation. As we saw in chapter 4 in the case of the Middle East, for years the United States followed a Hamiltonian policy that sought stability through support of autocrats and commerce, but in the end this did not prevent the rise of radical Islamist ideology and terrorism. The Wilsonians urge a transformational rather than a conservative or status quo foreign policy. In their view, without democratization, the Middle East (and other regions) will continue to be a breeding ground of rogue states and terrorist threats. Much of the debate inside the Bush administration over the Iraq War was between traditional Hamiltonian realists (such as Secretary of State Colin Powell) and a coalition of Jacksonians (such as Vice President Dick Cheney and Secretary of Defense Donald Rumsfeld) plus neoconservative Wilsonians (such as Deputy Defense Secretary Paul Wolfowitz). Part of the confusion over American objectives in going to war was that the administration used a variety of arguments that appealed to different camps. The suggestion of a connection to Al Qaeda and 9/11 was important to Jacksonians, who sought revenge and deterrence; the argument that Saddam Hussein was developing weapons of mass destruction in violation of UN resolutions appealed to Hamiltonians, and traditional Wilsonians in the Congress; and the need to remove a bloody dictator and transform Middle Eastern politics was important to the new Wilsonians.

In recent years, the Wilsonians have divided into two camps. President Woodrow Wilson, of course, was a Democrat, and traditional Wilsonians continue to stress both the promotion of democracy and the role of international institutions. The neoconservatives, many of whom split off from the Democratic Party after Vietnam, stress the importance of democracy, but drop Wilson's emphasis on international institutions. They do not want to be held back by institutional constraints and see our legitimacy coming from our focus on democracy. In that sense, the neoconservatives are advocates of soft power, but they focus too simply on substance and not enough on process. By downgrading the legitimacy that comes from institutional processes where others are consulted, they squander soft power.

Ironically, however, the only way to achieve the type of transformation that the neoconservatives seek is by working with others and avoiding the backlash that arises when the United States appears on the world stage as an imperial power acting unilaterally. What is more, since democracy cannot be imposed by force and requires a considerable time to take root, the most likely way to obtain staying power from the American public is through developing international legitimacy and burden sharing with allies and institutions. For Jacksonians such as Secretary of Defense Rumsfeld, this may not matter. They would prefer to punish the dictator and come home rather than engage in tedious nation building. In September 2003, Rumsfeld said of Iraq, "I don't believe it's our job to reconstruct the country."[30] But for serious neoconservatives, such as Deputy Defense Secretary Paul Wolfowitz, their impatience with international institutions and allies may undercut their own objectives. They understand the importance of soft power, but fail to appreciate all its dimensions and dynamics.

SOFT POWER AND POLICY

We saw earlier that soft power grows out of our culture, out of our domestic values and policies, and out of our foreign policy. Many of the effects of our culture, for better or for worse, are outside the control of government. But there is still a great deal that the government can do. We saw in chapter 4 that much more can be done to improve our public diplomacy in all dimensions. We can greatly improve our broadcast capabilities as well as our narrow-casting on the Internet. But both should be based on better listening as well. Newt Gingrich has written that "the impact and success of a new U.S. communication strategy should be measured continually on a country-by-country basis. An independent public affairs firm should report weekly on how U.S. messages are received in at least the world's 50 largest countries."[31] Such an approach would help us to select relevant themes as well as to fine-tune our short-term responses. And we should greatly increase our investment in soft power. We could easily afford to double the budget for public diplomacy, as well as raise its profile and direction from the White House.

Equally important will be to increase the exchanges across societies that allow our rich and diverse nongovernmental sectors to interact with those of other countries. It was a great mistake for the Clinton administration and the Congress to cut the budget and staff for cultural diplomacy and exchanges by nearly 30 percent after 1993.[32] And it is a mistake now to let visa policies curtail such contacts. The most effective communication often occurs not by means of distant broadcasts but in face-to-face contacts—what Edward R. Murrow called "the last three feet." In chapter 2 we saw how important cultural-exchange programs were in winning the Cold War. The best communicators are often not governments but civilians, both from the U.S. and from other countries.

We will need to be more inventive in this area, whether it be finding ways to improve the visa process for educational exchanges, encouraging more American students to study abroad, rethinking the role of the Peace Corps, inventing a major program for foreigners to teach their languages in American schools, starting a corporation for public diplomacy that will help tap into the resources of the private and nonprofit sectors, or a myriad of other ways. As Michael Holtzman has observed about the Middle East, our public diplomacy must acknowledge a world that is far more skeptical of government messages than we have assumed. "To be credible to the so-called Arab street, public diplomacy should be directed mainly at spheres of everyday life. Washington should put its money into helping American doctors, teachers, businesses, religious leaders, athletic teams, and entertainers go abroad and provide the sorts of services the people of the Middle East are eager for."[33]

As we saw in chapter 2, many of the social and political problems the United States has at home are shared with other postmodern societies, and so invidious comparisons do not seriously undercut our soft power. Moreover, we maintain strengths of openness, civil liberties, and democracy that appeal to others. Problems arise for our soft power when we do not live up to our own standards. As we struggle to find the right balance between freedom and security in the fight against terrorism, it is important to remember that others are watching as well. The Bush administration responded to human rights groups' accusations that it was torturing suspects by reaffirming its rejection of any techniques to interrogate suspects that would constitute 'cruel' treatment prohibited by the Constitution.[34]

Some domestic policies, such as capital punishment and the absence of gun controls, reduce the attractiveness of the United States in other countries, but are the results of differences in values that may persist for some time. Other policies, such as the refusal to discourage the production of gas-guzzling vehicles, damage the American reputation because they appear self-indulgent and demonstrate an unwillingness to consider the effects we are having on global climate change and other countries. Similarly, domestic agricultural subsidies that are structured to protect wealthy farmers while we preach the virtue of free markets to poor countries appear hypocritical in the eyes of others. In a democracy, the "dog" of domestic politics is often too large to be wagged by the "tail" of foreign policy, but when we ignore the connections between the two, our apparent hypocrisy is costly to our soft power.

The place where the government can do most in the near term to recover the recent American loss of soft power is by adjusting the style and substance of our foreign policy. Obviously there are times when foreign policies serve fundamental American interests and cannot and should not be changed. But tactics can often be adjusted without giving up basic interests. Style may be the easiest part. For one thing, the administration could go back to the wisdom about humility and warnings about arrogance that George W. Bush expressed in his 2000 campaign. There is no need to take pleasure in embarrassing allies, or to have a secretary of defense insulting them while a secretary of state is trying to woo them. As a British columnist wrote in the *Financial Times*, "I have a soft spot for Donald Rumsfeld. But as an ambassador for the American values so admired around the world, I can think of no one worse."[35] Prime Minister Tony Blair put it well in his 2003 address to the American Congress when he said that the real challenge for the United States now "is to show that this is a partnership built on persuasion, not command."[36]

On the substance of policy, the Bush administration deserves credit for its efforts to align the United States with the long-term aspirations of poor people in Africa and elsewhere through its Millennium Challenge initiative, which promises to increase aid to countries willing to make reforms, as well as its efforts to increase resources to combat AIDS and other infectious diseases. Success in implementing those programs will represent a significant investment in American soft power. So also will be the serious promotion of the peace process in the Middle East. National Security Adviser Condoleezza Rice has said, "America is a country that really does have to be committed to values and to making life better for people around the world. . . . It's not just the sword, it's the olive branch that speaks to those intentions."[37]

As for the sword, the United States will continue to need it from time to time in the struggle against terrorism and in our efforts to create stability. Maintaining our hard power is essential to security. But we will not succeed by the sword alone. Our doctrine of containment led to success in the Cold War not just because of military deterrence but because, as the famous diplomat George Kennan designed the policy, our soft power would help to transform the Soviet Bloc from within. Containment was not a static military doctrine but a transformational strategy, albeit one that took decades to accomplish. Indeed, Kennan frequently warned against what he regarded as the overmilitarization of containment and was a strong supporter of cultural contacts and exchanges. Those lessons about patience and the mixture of hard and soft power still stand us in good stead today.

When we do use our hard power, we will need to be more attentive to ways to make it less costly to our soft power by creating broad coalitions. Here the model should be the patient and painstaking work of George H. W. Bush in building the coalition for the first Gulf War. Those who write off "old Europe" as so enthralled by Venus that it is hopelessly opposed to the use of force should remember that 75 percent of the French and 63 percent of the German public supported the use of military force to free Kuwait before the Gulf War.[38] Similarly, both countries were active participants in NATO's use of military force against Serbia in the 1999 Kosovo War, despite the absence of a formal UN Security Council resolution. The difference was that in those two cases, American policy appeared legitimate. We had soft power, and were able to attract allies.

The UN is not the only source of legitimacy, and many people concluded that the Kosovo campaign was legitimate (though not formally legal) because it had the de facto support of a large majority of Security Council members. The UN is often an unwieldy institution. The veto power in the Security Council has meant that it has been able to authorize the use of force for a true collective-security operation only twice in half a century: in Korea and Kuwait. But it was designed to be a concert of large powers that would not work when they disagree. The veto is like a fuse box in the electrical system of a house. Better that the fuse blows and the lights go out than that the house burns down. Moreover, as Kofi Annan pointed out after the Kosovo War, the UN is torn between the traditional strict interpretation of state sovereignty and the rise of international humanitarian and human rights law that sets limits on what leaders can do to their citizens. Moreover, politics of consensus have made the United Nations Charter virtually impossible to amend. Nonetheless, for all its flaws, the UN has proved useful in its humanitarian and peacekeeping roles where states agree, and it remains an important source of legitimization in world politics.

The latter point is particularly galling to the new unilateralists, who correctly point to the undemocratic nature of many of the regimes that vote and chair committees. But their proposed solution of replacing the United Nations with a new organization of democracies ignores the fact that the major divisions over Iraq were among the democracies. Rather than engage in futile efforts at ignoring the UN or changing its architecture, we should improve our underlying bilateral diplomacy with the other major powers and use the UN in the practical ways in which it can help with the new strategy. In addition to the UN's development and humanitarian agenda, the Security Council may wind up playing a background role related to North Korea; the Committee on Terrorism can help to prod states to improve their procedures; and UN peacekeepers can save us from having to be the world's lone policeman. The UN can be useful to us in a variety of practical ways if we work at it; unilateralist attacks on it by Americans will backfire in a way that undercuts our soft power.

A MERICANS ARE STILL WORKING THEIR WAY through the aftermath of September 11. We are groping for a path through the strange new landscape created by technology and globalization whose dark aspects were vividly illuminated on that traumatic occasion. The Bush administration has correctly identified the nature of the new challenges that the nation faces and has reoriented American strategy accordingly. But the administration, like the Congress and the public, has been torn between different approaches to the implementation of the new strategy. The result has been a mixture of successes and failures. We have been more successful in the domain of hard power, where we have invested more, trained more, and have a clearer idea of what we are doing. We have been less successful in the areas of soft power, where our public diplomacy has been woefully inadequate and our neglect of allies and institutions has created a sense of illegitimacy that has squandered our attractiveness.

Yet this is ironic, because the United States is the country that is at the forefront of the information revolution as well as the country that built some of the longest-lasting alliances and institutions that the modern world has seen. We should know how to adapt and work with such institutions since they have been central to our power for more than half a century. And the United States is a country with a vibrant social and cultural life that provides an almost infinite number of points of contact with other societies. What's more, during the Cold War, we demonstrated that we know how to use the soft-power resources that our society produces.

It is time now for us to draw upon and combine our traditions in a different way. We need more Jefferson and less Jackson. Our Wilsonians are correct about the importance of the democratic transformation of world politics over the long term, but they need to remember the role of institutions and allies. They also need to temper their impatience with a good mixture of Hamiltonian realism. In short, America's success will depend upon our developing a deeper understanding of the role of soft power and developing a better balance of hard and soft power in our foreign policy. That will be smart power. We have done it before; we can do it again.

Notes

PREFACE

1. "Soft and Hard Power," CBS News, January 28, 2003, available at: http://www.cbsnews.com/stories/2003/01/28/opinion/diplomatic/main538 320.shtml. See also Steven Weisman, "He Denies It, but Powell Appears to Have Gotten Tougher," *International Herald Tribune*, January 29, 2003, p. 5.

2. "Old Softie," *Financial Times*, September 30, 2003, p. 17.

3. John Barry and Evan Thomas, "Dissent in the Bunker," *Newsweek*, December 15, 2003, p. 36.

4. Matthew Purdy, "After the War, New Stature for Rumsfeld," *New York Times*, April 20, 2003, p. A1.

5. Wesley K. Clark, *Winning Modern Wars: Iraq, Terrorism, and the American Empire* (New York: PublicAffairs, 2003), p. 182.

6. "A Famous Victory and a Tough Sequel," *Financial Times*, April 10, 2003, p. 12.

CHAPTER 1:
THE CHANGING NATURE OF POWER

1. Robert Dahl, *Who Governs? Democracy and Power in an American City* (New Haven: Yale University Press, 1961).

2. David Baldwin, "Power Analysis and World Politics: New Trends versus Old Tendencies," *World Politics* 31, 2 (January 1979), pp. 161–94.

3. Ibid., p. 164b.

4. A. J. P. Taylor, *The Struggle for Mastery in Europe, 1848–1918* (Oxford: Oxford University Press, 1954), p. xxix.

5. I first introduced this concept in *Bound to Lead: The Changing Nature of American Power* (New York: Basic Books, 1990), chapter 2. It builds on what Peter Bachrach and Morton Baratz called the "second face of power." See their "Decisions and Nondecisions: An Analytical Framework," *American Political Science Review* (September 1963), pp. 632–42.

6. I am indebted to Mark Moore for pointing this out to me.

7. See Jane J. Mansbridge, *Beyond Self-Interest* (Chicago: University of Chicago Press, 1990).

8. Repulsion and hatred can also move people to act, but the outcomes they produce are usually not desired by those who generate them. While some might consider repulsion a form of "negative soft power," such a term would be inconsistent with my definition of power as the capacity to produce desired outcomes. Thus I use the term "repulsion" as the opposite of "attraction."

9. Hubert Védrine with Dominique Moisi, *France in an Age of Globalization* (Washington, D.C.: Brookings Institution Press, 2001), p. 3.

10. E. H. Carr, *The Twenty Years' Crisis, 1919–1939: An Introduction to the Study of International Relations* (New York: Harper & Row, 1964), p. 108.

11. John McCloy and Arthur Schlesinger, Jr., quoted in Mark Haefele, "John F. Kennedy, USIA, and World Public Opinion," *Diplomatic History* 25, 1 (Winter 2001), p. 66.

12. Ibid., p. 75. See also USIA data in Richard L. Merritt and Donald J. Puchala, *Western European Perspectives on International Affairs* (New York: Frederick A. Praeger, 1968), pp. 513–38.

13. John P. Vloyantes, *Silk Glove Hegemony: Finnish-Soviet Relations, 1944–1974* (Kent, Ohio: Kent State University Press, 1975) uses the term "soft sphere of influence."

14. Frank Bruni, "A Nation That Exports Oil, Herring and Peace," *New York Times*, December 21, 2002, p. A3.

15. Michael Ignatieff, "Canada in the Age of Terror—Multilateralism Meets a Moment of Truth," *Options Politiques*, February 2003, p. 16.

16. Jehangir Pocha, "The Rising Soft Power of India and China," *New Perspectives Quarterly* 20 (Winter 2003), p. 9.

17. Josef Joffe, "Who's Afraid of Mr. Big?" *The National Interest*, Summer 2001, p. 43.

18. Niall Ferguson, "Think Again: Power," *Foreign Policy*, January–February 2003.

19. Neal M. Rosendorf, "Social and Cultural Globalization: Concepts, History, and America's Role," in Joseph Nye and John D. Donahue, eds., *Governance in a Globalizing World* (Washington, D.C.: Brookings Institution Press, 2000), p. 123.

20. Todd Gitlin, "Taking the World by (Cultural) Force," *The Straits Times* (Singapore), January 11, 1999, p. 2.

21. Elisabeth Rosenthal, "Chinese Test New Weapon from West: Lawsuits," *New York Times*, June 16, 2001, p. A3.

22. Pew Global Attitudes Project, *Views of a Changing World June 2003* (Washington, D.C.: Pew Research Center for the People and the Press, 2003), pp. 22–23.

23. For an early example, see John R. P. French and Bertram Raven, "Bases of Social Power," in Dorwin Cartwright and Alvin Zander, eds., *Group Dynamics: Reseach and Theory*, 3rd ed. (New York: Harper & Row, 1968), pp. 259–69.

24. This builds on a distinction first made by Arnold Wolfers, *Discord and Collaboration: Essays on International Politics* (Baltimore: Johns Hopkins University Press, 1962).

25. Ibid.

26. Milos Forman, "Red Spring Episode 14: The Sixties," interview, available at: http://www.gwu.edu/~nsarchiv/coldwar/interviews/episode-14/forman1.html. Quoted in Matthew Kohut, "The Role of American Soft Power in the Democratization of Czechoslovakia," unpublished paper, April 2003.

27. Whether this would change with the proliferation of nuclear weapons to more states is hotly debated among theorists. Deterrence should work with most states, but the prospects of accident and loss of control would increase. For my views, see Joseph Nye, *Nuclear Ethics* (New York: Free Press, 1986).

28. John Meuller, *Retreat from Doomsday: The Obsolescence of Major War* (New York: Basic Books, 1989).

29. Robert Cooper, *The Postmodern State and the World Order* (London: Demos, 2000), p. 22.

30. Robert Kagan, *Of Paradise and Power* (New York: Knopf, 2003).

31. Thomas Friedman, *The Lexus and the Olive Tree: Understanding Globalization* (New York: Farrar Straus and Giroux, 1999), chapter 6.

32. Richard N. Rosecrance, *The Rise of the Trading State* (New York: Basic Books, 1986), pp. 16, 160.

33. John Arquilla and David Ronfeldt, *The Emergence of Neopolitik: Toward an American Information Strategy* (Santa Monica: RAND Corporation, 1999), p. 42.

34. National Research Council, *Making the Nation Safer* (Washington, D.C.: National Academies Press, 2002), p. 25.

35. For details see Joseph Nye, *The Paradox of American Power* (New York: Oxford University Press, 2002), chapter 2.

36. Walter Laquer, "Left, Right and Beyond: The Changing Face of Terror," in James Hoge and Gideon Rose, eds., *How Did This Happen?* (New York: PublicAffairs, 2001), p. 74.

37. Haefele, "John F. Kennedy, USIA, and World Public Opinion," p. 78.

38. Cathy Horyn, "Macho America Storms Europe's Runways," *New York Times*, July 3, 2003, p. 1.

39. Quoted in "Special Report Al Qaeda," *The Economist*, March 8, 2003, p. 25.

40. Evan Thomas, "Road to War," *Newsweek*, March 21, 2003, p. 60.

41. William Kristol and Lawrence Kaplan, *The War over Iraq: Saddam's Tyranny and America's Mission* (San Francisco: Encounter Books, 2003), p. 112.

42. Charles Krauthammer, "The French Challenge," *Washington Post*, February 21, 2003, p. 27.

43. Robert A. Pape, "The World Pushes Back," *Boston Sunday Globe*, March 23, 2003, p. H1.

44. Fareed Zakaria, "And Now, Global Booby Prizes," *Newsweek*, September 29, 2003, p. 13.

45. Lael Brainard and Michael O'Hanlon, "The Heavy Price of America's Going It Alone," *Financial Times*, August 6, 2003, p. 13.

46. Paul Richter, "U.S. Enlists More Countries in Iraq, at Taxpayers' Expense," *Los Angeles Times*, June 22, 2003, p. 3.

47. David Gelernter, "Replacing the United Nations to Make Way for the Big Three," *Weekly Standard*, March 17, 2003.

48. Jennifer Lee, "How Protesters Mobilized So Many and So Nimbly," *New York Times*, February 23, 2003, The Week in Review, p. 4.

49. For various views of what it means, see "What Is the International Community?" *Foreign Policy*, September 2002.

50. Bill Keller, "Does Not Play Well with Others," *New York Times*, June 22, 2003, Book Review, p. 9.

51. Mustafa al-Feqi quoted in Susan Sachs, "Arab Foreign Ministers Urge US Withdrawal," *New York Times*, March 25, 2003, p. B11.

52. "US Invasion Pushes Pakistani Elite Closer to Hardline Islam," *Financial Times*, March 28, 2003, p. 1.

53. Don Van Natta, Jr., and Desmond Butler, "Anger on Iraq Seen as New Qaeda Recruiting Tool," *New York Times*, March 16, 2003, p. 1. Their conclusion is reinforced by the judgment of the authors of the report "Strategic Balance" (London: International Institute of Strategic Studies, 2003).

54. Pew Global Attitudes Project, *Views of a Changing World*.

55. "Wielder of Mass Deception?" *The Economist*, October 4, 2003, p. 13.

56. Seung Hwan Kim, "Anti-Americanism in Korea," *The Washington Quarterly*, Winter 2002–3, p. 116.

57. See Cooper, *Postmodern State*, and Daniel Bell, *The Coming of Post-Industrial Society: A Venture in Social Forecasting* (1976; paperback edition with new foreword: New York: Basic Books, 1999), foreword, passim.

CHAPTER 2:
SOURCES OF AMERICAN SOFT POWER

1. Philip Coggan, "Uncle Sam Stands Above the Rest," *Financial Times*, FT Report–FT 500, p. 3.

2. "The 100 Top Brands," *Business Week*, August 4, 2003, pp. 72–78. Also available at: http://www.brandchannel.com/images/home/bgb_2003. pdf; "Financial Times Releases 5th Annual International MBA Survey," Business Wire (online magazine), January 20, 2003.

3. Data compiled from the World Bank's "World Development Indicators" database.

4. Neal M. Rosendorf, "Social and Cultural Globalization: Concepts, History, and America's Role," in Joseph Nye and John Donahue, eds., *Governance in a Globalizing World* (Washington, D.C.: Brookings Institution Press, 2000), pp. 109–34.

5. Alan Riding, "The New EU," *New York Times*, January 12, 2003, Education Life section, p. 30.

6. Hey-Kyung Koh, ed., *Open Doors 2002: Report of International Educational Exchange* (New York: Institute of International Education, 2002), p. 22.

7. Statistics from Economist Books, ed., *Pocket World in Figures 2003 Edition* (London: Profile Books, Ltd., 2003), pp. 90–92, except the statistics on scientific publications, which were compiled from data in the World Bank's "World Development Indicators" database.

8. "Norway Tops Quality of Life Index," *New York Times*, July 9, 2003, p. A6.

9. Economist Books, ed., *Pocket World in Figures 2003 Edition* (London: Profile Books, 2003), p. 95.

10. Pew Global Attitudes Project, *Views of a Changing World June 2003* (Washington, D.C.: Pew Research Center for the People and the Press, 2003), pp. 19, T132–34.

11. Ibid., pp. 19–23.

12. See Leo Crespi, "Trend Measurement of US Standing in Foreign Public Opinion," United States Information Agency manuscript, June 1, 1978 (available by request from the National Archives: www.nara.gov), charts 2–5; and Steven K. Smith and Douglas Wertman, *US–West European Relations During the Reagan Years* (London: Macmillan, 1992), pp. 92–93.

13. Thomas Alan Schwartz, *Lyndon Johnson and Europe* (Cambridge: Harvard University Press, 2003), p. 85.

14. Jerry Adler et al., "What the World Thinks of America," *Newsweek*, July 11, 1983, p. 44, discussing Gallup poll conducted for *Newsweek*.

15. James Ceaser, "A Genealogy of Anti-Americanism," *The Public Interest*, Summer 2003.

16. Simon Schama, "The Unloved American," *The New Yorker*, March 10, 2003, p. 34.

17. Reinhold Wagnleitner and Elaine Tyler May, eds., *"Here, There and Everywhere": The Foreign Politics of American Popular Culture* (Hanover: University Press of New England, 2000), p. 6.

18. John Trumpbour, "Hollywood and the Decline of European Empire," in Elisabeth Kraut and Caroline Auer, eds., *Simulacrum America* (Rochester, N.Y.: Camden House, 2000), pp. 206–8.

19. "Over Here," *The Economist*, March 15, 2003, p. 54.

20. Leo P. Crespi, "Trends in the Image of U.S. Strength in Foreign Public Opinion," United States Information Agency, Office of Research, January 28, 1977, p. 13.

21. John Burns, "Amid Serbia's Battle Cries, Old Voice of Dissent," *New York Times*, March 27, 1992, p. 4; Joseph Nye, "Manage Japan, Don't Compete with It," *Wall Street Journal*, January 17, 1991, p. A10.

22. Pew Global Attitudes Project, *What the World Thinks in 2002* (Washington, D.C.: Pew Research Center for the People and the Press, 2002), p. T54.

23. Roger Cohen, "Fearful over the Future, Europe Seizes on Food," *New York Times*, August 29, 1999, section 4, p. l.

24. "Iranian, in Paris Speech, Aims a Barb at U.S.," *New York Times*, October 29, 1999, p. A8.

25. Quoted in Walter LaFeber, *Michael Jordan and the New Global Capitalism* (New York: Norton, 1999), p. 20.

26. Barbara Wallraff, "What Global Language?" *The Atlantic Monthly*, November 2000.

27. Michael Elliott, "A Target Too Good to Resist," *Newsweek*, January 31, 2000, pp. 27–28.

28. Neil Buckley, "Eyes on the Fries," *Financial Times*, August 29, 2003, p. 9.

29. See Neal M. Rosendorf, "The Life and Times of Samuel Bronston, Builder of Hollywood in Madrid: A Study in the International Scope and Influence of American Popular Culture," Ph.D. dissertation, Harvard University, 2000, "Appendix: The Power of American Pop Culture—Evolution of an Elitist Critique," pp. 402–15 and passim.

30. Arendt quoted in Michael Ermath, "German Unification as Self-Inflicted Americanization," in Wagnleitner and May, *"Here, There and Everywhere,"* p. 267.

31. Nosa Owens-Ibie, "Programmed for Domination," in Wagnleitner and May, *"Here, There, and Everywhere,"* p. 141.

32. Masako Notoji, "Cultural Transformation of John Philip Sousa and

Disneyland in Japan," in Wagnleitner and May, *"Here, There, and Everywhere,"* p. 225.

33. Steven Weisman, "U.S. Must Counteract Image in Muslim World, Panel Says," *New York Times,* October 1, 2003, p. 1.

34. Pew Global Attitudes Project, *What the World Thinks in 2002,* pp. T54–T58.

35. United Nations Development Programme, "Arab Human Development Report 2003," available at: http://www.undp.org/rbas/ahdr/english 2003.html.

36. Fouad Ajami, "The Falseness of Anti-Americanism," *Foreign Policy,* September-October 2003, pp. 58, 61.

37. Mamoun Fandy, "The Iraq the Arab World Saw All Along," *New York Times,* April 10, 2003, p. A27.

38. See Andrew Kohut, *Wall Street Journal,* letter to the editor, July 10, 2003.

39. Institute for Research: Middle Eastern Policy, "Dividends of Fear: America's $94 Billion Arab Market Loss," June 30, 2003, available at: http://www.irmep.org/Policy_Briefs/6_30_2003_DOF.html.

40. Quoted in Thomas Friedman, "Is Google God?" *New York Times,* June 29, 2003, The Week in Review, p. 13.

41. Colin Powell, "Statement on International Education Week 2001," available at: http://www.state.gov/secretary/rm/2001/4462.htm.

42. Association of International Educators, "In America's Interest: Welcoming International Students," available at: http://www.nafsa.org/content/PublicPolicy/stf/inamericasinterest.htm, p. 5.

43. Kennan, Eisenhower, and musician are quoted in Yale Richmond, *Cultural Exchange and the Cold War* (University Park: Pennsylvania State University Press, 2003), pp. 123, 124, 127.

44. Ibid., pp. 22–32.

45. Edward Rothstein, "Damning (Yet Desiring) Mickey and the Big Mac," *New York Times,* March 2, 2002, p. A17.

46. Ben Wattenberg, *The First Universal Nation* (New York: Free Press, 1991), p. 213.

47. Carl Sandburg, quoted in Reinhold Wagnleitner, *Coca-Colonization and the Cold War* (Chapel Hill: University of North Carolina Press, 1994), p. 222.

48. Charles P. Pierce, "The Goodwill Games," *Boston Globe*, September 21, 2003.

49. Matthew Collin, *Guerrilla Radio* (New York: Nation Books, 2001), p. 41.

50. John Fraim, *Battle of Symbols: Emerging Global Dynamics* (Enfield, U.K.: Daimon, 2003), chapter 8.

51. Saritha Rai, "Tastes of India in U.S. Wrappers," *New York Times*, April 29, 2003, p. W1.

52. John Tagliabue, "U.S. Brands Abroad Are Feeling Global Tension," *New York Times*, March 15, 2003, p. B3.

53. Rob Kroes, "American Empire and Cultural Imperialism: A View from the Receiving End," *Diplomatic History* 29 (Summer 1999), pp. 468–74.

54. Reinhold Wagnleitner, "The Empire of Fun, or Talkin' Soviet Union Blues: The Sound of Freedom and U.S. Cultural Hegemony in Europe," *Diplomatic History* 23 (Summer 1999), p. 515.

55. For evidence of the Soviet loss of soft power in Czechoslovakia after the Prague Spring crackdown, see Radio Free Europe, Audience and Public Opinion Research Department, *Czech and Slovak Self-Image and the Czech and Slovak Image of the Americans, Germans, Russians, and Chinese* (Munich: Radio Free Europe, 1970), p. 67.

56. Richmond, *Cultural Exchange and the Cold War*, pp. 128–131, 162, 205.

57. This paragraph is based on Matthew Kohut, "The Role of American Soft Power in the Democratization of Czechoslovakia," unpublished paper, April 2003, Kennedy School of Government.

58. Wagnleitner, "Empire of Fun," p. 506.

59. "TV Finally Approved by South Africa," *New York Times*, April 28, 1971.

60. Peter Waldman, "Iran Fights New Foe: Western Television," *Wall Street Journal*, August 8, 1994, p. 10.

61. "Prodding the Clerics," *The Economist*, July 12, 2003, p. 24.

62. Azar Nafisi, "The Books of Revolution," *Wall Street Journal*, June 18, 2003.

63. Jehangir Pocha, "The Rising Soft Power of India and China," *New Perspectives Quarterly* 20 (Winter 2003), p. 6; Rick Lyman, "China Is Warming to Hollywood's Glow," *New York Times*, September 18, 2003, p. B1.

64. Wagnleitner, *Coca-Colonization*, p. xi.

65. Gulriz Buken, "Backlash: An Argument against the Spread of American Popular Culture in Turkey," in Wagnleitner and May, *"Here, There and Everywhere,"* p. 248b.

66. Meena Janardham, "Mideast: U.S. May Be Unpopular, but Students Still Head for It," Interpress Service, available at: http://www.ipsnews.net, accessed January 20, 2003.

67. Neal Gabler, "The World Still Watches America," *New York Times,* January 9, 2003, p. A27.

68. Suzanne Kapner, "U.S. TV Shows Losing Potency Around World," *New York Times,* January 2, 2003, p. 1; "Anti-Americanism and Television," *The Economist,* April 5, 2003, p. 59.

69. John G. Blair, "First Steps Toward Globalization," in Wagnleitner and May, *"Here, There and Everywhere,"* p. 27.

70. Jo Johnson, "Paris Deputies in Tune with Plans for State to Fund 24-Hour 'French CNN,'" *Financial Times,* May 15, 2003, p. 10.

71. J. Mitchell Jaffee and Gabriel Weimann, "The New Lord of the Global Village?," in Wagnleitner and May, *"Here, There and Everywhere,"* p. 291.

72. Richard Tomkins, "Happy Birthday, Globalisation," *Financial Times,* May 6, 2003, p. 8.

73. Personal communication, June 2003.

74. Jim Yardley, "Training Site Is Questioned About Links to Hijackers," *New York Times,* September 14, 2001, p. 4.

75. Jianying Zha, "Saddam Hussein as Surrogate Dictator," *New York Times,* April 8, 2003, p. 31.

76. Times-Mirror Center for the People and the Press, "East-West Poll," 1991 (available from the Pew Research Center, www.people-press.org.).

77. German Marshall Fund, Transatlantic Trends 2003, "Topline Data," available at: http://www.transatlantictrends.org, p. 49.

78. Pew Global Attitudes Project, *What the World Thinks in 2002,* p. T55.

79. Smith and Wertman, *US–West European Relations During the Reagan Years,* p. 108.

80. Derek Bok, *The State of the Nation* (Cambridge, Mass.: Harvard University Press, 1996), p. 359.

81. Gregg Easterbrook, "America the O.K.," *The New Republic,* January 4, 1999, pp. 19–25.

82. David Whitman, *The Optimism Gap: The I'm OK—They're Not Syndrome and the Myth of American Decline* (New York: Walker, 1998), p. 92.

83. Suzanne Garment, *Scandal: The Culture of Mistrust in American Politics* (New York: Doubleday, 1991).

84. Steven Holmes, "Defying Forecasts, Census Response Ends Declining Trend," *New York Times,* September 20, 2000, p. 23.

85. Richard Berke, "Nonvoters Are No More Alienated Than Voters, a Survey Shows," *New York Times,* May 30, 1996, p. A21; "Conventions and Their Enemies," *The Economist,* July 22, 2000, p. 34.

86. See Joseph Nye, Philip D. Zelikow, and David C. King, eds., *Why People Don't Trust Government* (Cambridge, Mass.: Harvard University Press, 1997), chapters 9, 10, and "Conclusion"; see also Pippa Norris, ed., *Critical Citizens: Global Support for Democratic Government* (New York: Oxford University Press, 1999).

87. Pew Partnership for Civic Change, "New Survey Dispels Myths on Citizen Engagement," available at: http://www.pew-partnership.org.

88. Robert Putnam, *Bowling Alone: The Collapse and Revival of American Community* (New York: Simon & Schuster, 2000), p. 48.

89. Public Policy Institute of California, "Silicon Valley's Skilled Immigrants: Generating Jobs and Wealth for California," *Research Brief Issue 21,* June 1999, p. 2.

90. Tamar Lewin, "Family Decay Global, Study Says," *New York Times,* May 30, 1995, p. 5.

91. Bok, *State of the Nation,* p. 376.

92. Pew Research Center for the People and the Press, "Bush Unpopular in Europe, Seen as Unilateralist," available at: http://people-press.org/reports/display.php3?ReportID=5, accessed August 15, 2001.

93. Laurie Goodstein, "Seeing Islam as Evil Faith, Evangelicals Seek Converts," *New York Times,* May 27, 2003, p. 1.

94. Laurie Goodstein, "Top Evangelicals Critical of Colleagues over Islam," *New York Times,* May 8, 2003, p. 22.

95. Irene Kahn, quoted in Sarah Lyall, "Amnesty Calls World Less Safe," *New York Times,* May 20, 2003, p. 14; Kenneth Roth, quoted in Bernard Wysocki, Jr., and Jess Bravin, "Issue of Guantanamo Captives'

Treatment Resurfaces—As U.S. Complains About Iraqi Conduct, Human-Rights Groups Charge Hypocrisy," *Wall Street Journal*, April 1, 2003, p. A4.

96. "America the Scary Bends Democracy," *Financial Times*, June 9,2003, p. 14; "Unjust, Unwise, UnAmerican," *The Economist*, July 12, 2003, p. 9.

97. Geir Lundestad, *Empire by Integration: The United States and European Integration, 1945–1997* (New York: Oxford University Press, 1998), p. 155.

98. For a full discussion of the complexity and problems of definition, see Inge Kaul, Isabelle Grunberg, and Marc A. Stern, eds., *Global Public Goods: International Cooperation in the 21st Century* (New York: Oxford University Press, 1999). Strictly defined, public goods are those whose use is nonrivalrous and nonexclusionary.

99. "Economic Focus: Gauging Generosity," *The Economist*, May 3, 2003, p. 72.

100. Richard Bernstein, "To Butt In or Not in Human Rights: The Gap Narrows," *New York Times*, August 4, 2001, p. 15.

101. Steven Mufson, "Bush Nudged by the Right over Rights," *International Herald Tribune*, January 27–28, 2001, p. 3. See also "American Power—For What? A Symposium," *Commentary*, January 2000, p. 21n.

102. Lawrence F. Kaplan and William Kristol, "Neither a Realist nor a Liberal, W. is a Liberator," *Wall Street Journal Europe*, January 30, 2003, p. A8.

103. Charles Krauthammer, "The New Unilateralism," *Washington Post*, June 8, 2001, p. A29.

104. Robert Kagan and William Kristol, "The Present Danger," *The National Interest*, Spring 2000, pp. 58, 64, 67.

105. Charles Krauthammer, "The New Unilateralism," *Washington Post*, June 8, 2001, p. A29.

106. Kagan and Kristol, "Present Danger," p. 67.

107. Robert W. Tucker, in "American Power—For What? A Symposium," *Commentary*, January 2000, p. 46.

108. Pew Research Center for the People and the Press, "Bush Unpopular in Europe." Gallup International Association, "Post War Iraq Poll," May 2003, available at: http://www.gallup-international.com.

109. German Marshall Fund, Transatlantic Trends 2003, "Topline Data," "Survey Results," pp. 19–21.

110. John Ikenberry, "Getting Hegemony Right," *The National Interest*, Spring 2001, pp. 17–24.

111. Stephen Holden, "Revisiting McNamara and the War He Headed," *New York Times*, October 11, 2003, p. 23.

112. Eric Schmitt, "Cheney Lashes Out at Critics on Iraq," *New York Times*, October 11, 2003, p. 1b.

113. German Marshall Fund, Transatlantic Trends 2003, "Topline Data," p. 24.

114. Ibid., p. 21.

115. Thom Shanker, "U.S. Commander in Iraq Says New Troops May Be Needed to Combat 'Guerrilla' War," *New York Times*, July 17, 2003, p. 1.

116. "2nd Presidential Debate Between Gov. Bush and Vice President Gore," *New York Times*, October 12, 2000, p. A20.

117. "Roger Cohen, "Arrogant or Humble? Bush Encounters Europeans' Hostility," *International Herald Tribune*, May 8, 2001, p. 1. Among the multilateral agreements that the administration opposed in its first six months were the International Criminal Court, the Comprehensive Test Ban Treaty, the ABM Treaty, the Kyoto Protocol, a Small Arms Control Pact, a Biological Weapons Protocol, and an OECD measure to control tax havens. "By knocking off several of the hard-earned, high-profile treaties on arms control and the environment, Mr. Bush has been subjected to outrage from some of America's closest friends—who wonder what will replace a world ordered by treaties—as well as its adversaries who see arrogance in Mr. Bush's actions" (Thom Shanker, "White House Says US Is Not a Loner, Just Choosy," *New York Times*, July 31, 2001, p. 1).

118. Audrey Woods, "U.S. Is Arrogant, Poll in 11 Nations Says Bush Got Unfavorable Ratings Among 58 Percent of Those Questioned for the BBC," *Philadelphia Inquirer*, June 19, 2003, p. A8.

119. Philip Stephens, "The World Needs a Confident America, Not a Fearful One," *Financial Times*, December 13, 2002, p. 21.

120. Irwin Stelzer, "America Is Needlessly Scaring Its Friends Away," *The Times (London)*, June 3, 2003, p. 16.

121. Richard Cohen describes John Bolton in "But Still Ruffling Feathers," *Washington Post*, June 17, 2003, p. 21.

122. James Harding, "Conflicting Views from Two Bush Camps," *Financial Times*, March 20, 2003.

CHAPTER 3:
OTHERS' SOFT POWER

1. Richard L. Merritt and Donald J. Puchala, *Western European Perspectives on International Affairs* (New York: Frederick A. Praeger, 1968), pp. 513, 534–35, citing United States Information Agency surveys.

2. Ibid., pp. 243–49; Steven K. Smith and Douglas A. Wertman, *US–West European Relations During the Reagan Years* (London: Macmillan, 1992), pp. 98, 275–77.

3. Central Intelligence Agency, *The World Factbook*, available online at: http://www.cia.gov/cia/publications/factbook/fields/2098.html. The five most widely spoken European languages are English, Spanish, Portuguese, Russian, and German.

4. Craig Whitney, "French Speakers Meet Where Few Will Hear," *New York Times*, November 15, 1997, p. 4; Eric Teo, "Soft Power Lessons for Singapore from the French," *Business Times (Singapore)*, September 19, 2002.

5. Seth Mydans, "In a Contest of Cultures, East Embraces West," *New York Times*, March 12, 2003, p. A4.

6. Economist Books, *Pocket World in Figures 2003* (London: Profile Books), pp. 15, 41, 73, 76, 90–92.

7. Pew Global Attitudes Project, *What the World Thinks in 2002* (Washington, D.C.: Pew Research Center for the People and the Press, 2003), p. T44; Chicago Council on Foreign Relations and the German Marshall Fund, Worldviews 2002, "Transatlantic Key Findings Topline Data," available at: http://www.worldviews.org/questionnaires/transatlantic_questionnaire.pdf, p. 21.

8. Rüdiger Meyenberg and Henk Dekker, eds., *Perceptions of Europe in East and West* (Oldenburg, Germany: Bibliotheks- und Informationssystem der Universität Oldenburg, 1992), pp. 70, 50.

9. Matthew Kohut, "The Role of American Soft Power in the Democratization of Czechoslovakia," unpublished paper, April 2003, Kennedy School of Government, pp. 11–12.

10. European Commission, Eurobarometer, Eurobarometer Surveys, Candidate Countries Eurobarometer, Spring 2003, available at: http://europa.eu.int/comm/public_opinion/archives/cceb/2003/CCEB_2003.3_candidates.pdf.

11. Timothy Garton Ash, "The Great Divide," *Prospect Magazine*, March 2003.

12. Elaine Sciolino, "European Union Turns Down Turkey's Bid for Membership," *New York Times*, December 13, 2002, p. A16.

13. European Commission, Eurobarometer, Candidate Countries Eurobarometer, Spring 2003.

14. Shirley Williams, "Soft Europe Must Come Into Its Own," *Independent on Sunday*, April 13, 2003, p. 22.

15. German Marshall Fund and Compagnia di San Paulo, Transatlantic Trends 2003, "Topline Data," "Survey Results—Topline Data," p. 47.

16. William Frey, quoted in Richard Bernstein, "An Aging Europe May Find Itself on the Sidelines," *New York Times*, June 29, 2003, section 1, p. 3. For further information about world demographic trends, see *The Economist*, "Half a Billion Americans?" August 22, 2002.

17. Frederick Schauer, "The Politics and Incentives of Legal Transplantation," in Joseph Nye and John Donahue, eds., *Governance in a Globalizing World* (Washington, D.C.: Brookings Institution Press, 2000), p. 257.

18. "Desperately Seeking a Perfect Model," *The Economist*, April 10, 1999, pp. 67–68.

19. Even as sympathetic an observer as Martin Wolf of the *Financial Times* notes ("The Lure of the American Way," *Financial Times*, November 1, 2000, p. 25),"Some of the most successful economies, in terms of high technology and low unemployment (though with a mixed record of productivity growth) have been the Nordic welfare states. Yet these are in some respects the polar opposites of the US, notably on taxation and public spending. For all its success, it is unlikely that the US offers the only workable way to organize an advanced economy."

20. Times-Mirror Center for the People and the Press, "East-West Poll," 1991, available from the Pew Research Center, www.people-press.org.

21. Andrew Moravcsik, "How Europe Can Win Without an Army," *Financial Times*, April 3, 2003.

22. Jack Straw, "Don't Write Off Europe's Global Role: Beyond the Broken Crockery," *International Herald Tribune*, March 27, 2003, p. 10.

23. Moravscik, "How Europe Can Win Without an Army."

24. "The Tortoise and the Hare," *The Economist*, March 14, 2002.

25. Margaret Wyszomirski, Christopher Burgess, and Catherine Peila, "International Cultural Relations: A Multi-Country Comparison," April 2003, Ohio State University, available at: http://www.culturalpolicy.org/pdf/MJWpaper.pdf, p. 19.

26. Philip Stephens, "The Transatlantic Alliance Is Worse Off Than the Coalition," *Financial Times*, March 28, 2003, p. 21.

27. Asian Development Bank, *Emerging Asia* (Manila: Asian Development Bank, 1997), p. 11.

28. Koh Buck Song, "The Trick that S'pore Missed: It Has Failed to Harness Soft Power," *Today* (Singapore), August 20, 2003, p. 28.

29. John Lennon, quoted in Jehangir Pocha, "The Rising 'Soft Power' of India and China," *New Perspectives Quarterly* 20 (Winter 2003), p. 6.

30. Mohamad Rusli, quoted in David Sanger, "Power of the Yen Winning Asia," *New York Times*, December 5, 1991, p. D1.

31. Mydans, "In a Contest of Cultures, East Embraces West."

32. Ibid.

33. "Corporate, Maybe: But Governance?" *The Economist*, June 21, 2003, p. 11.

34. Economist Books, *Pocket World in Figures 2003* (London: Profile Books, 2003), pp. 76, 91.

35. "Special Report: The Top 100 Brands," *Businessweek*, August 4, 2003, pp. 73–74.

36. Douglas McGray, "Japan's Gross National Cool," *Foreign Policy*, May-June 2002, p. 47.

37. Ibid.

38. Margaret Talbot, "Pokemon Hegemon," *The New York Times Magazine*, December 15, 2002, p. 112.

39. Elizabeth Hastings and Philip Hastings, eds., *Index to International Public Opinion, 1996–1997* (Westport, Conn.: Greenwood Press, 1998), p. 609, citing *Yomiuri Shimbun* poll.

40. *Newsweek* poll, released January 10, 2001. Results compiled from Polling the Nation database.

41. Howard French, "Insular Japan Needs, but Resists, Immigration," *New York Times*, July 24, 2003, p. 24.

42. Prime Minister's Commission, *The Frontier Within* (Tokyo: Cabinet Secretariat, 2000).

43. Hisashi Owada, "The Shaping of World Public Order and the Role of Japan," *Japan Review of International Affairs*, Spring 2000, p. 11.

44. Jerome C. Glenn, "Japan: Cultural Power of the Future," *Nikkei Weekly*, December 7, 1992, p. 7.

45. "Multinational Movies: Questions on Politics," *New York Times*, November 27, 1990, p. D7.

46. "Japanese News Media Join Export Drive," *International Herald Tribune*, May 10, 1991; Teresa Watanabe, "Japanese Media Try to Export Coverage," *Los Angeles Times*, May 6, 1991, p. 6; David Sanger, "NHK of Japan Ends Plan for Global News Service," *New York Times*, December 9, 1991, p. D8.

47. Calvin Sims, "Japan Beckons and East Asia's Youth Fall in Love," *New York Times*, December 5, 1999, p. A3; "Advance of the Amazonesu," *The Economist*, July 22, 2000, p. 61.

48. Pocha, "The Rising 'Soft Power' of India and China."

49. "Thailand's Gastro-diplomacy," *The Economist*, February 23, 2002, p. 48.

50. European Commission, Eurobarometers 14, pp. 39–56; 25, pp. 26–46; 33, pp. 43–46; 46, pp. 40–44 and B.46. All Eurobarometers available at: http://europa.eu.int/comm/public_opinion/archives/eb_arch_en.htm.

51. Schauer, "Politics and Incentives of Legal Transplantation," p. 258.

52. Ann Florini, ed., *The Third Force: The Rise of Transnational Civil Society* (Washington, D.C.: Carnegie Endowment, 2000), chapter 1; Margaret E. Keck and Kathryn Sikkink, *Activists Beyond Borders: Advocacy Networks in International Politics* (Ithaca, N.Y.: Cornell University Press, 1998), chapter 2; James N. Rosenau, *Turbulence in World Politics: A Theory of Change and Continuity* (Princeton, N.J.: Princeton University Press, 1990), p. 409; "The Non-Governmental Order," *The Economist*, December 11, 1999.

53. Michael Edwards, *NGO Rights and Responsibilities* (London: Foreign Policy Centre, 2000); Florini, *Third Force;* Jessica T. Mathews, "Power Shift," *Foreign Affairs*, January/February 1997, p. 50.

54. Marlies Glasius, Mary Kaldor, and Helmut Anheier, eds., *Global Civil Society 2002* (New York: Oxford University Press, 2002), p. 6.

55. Factiva–Dow Jones database, searched between January 14 and January 25, 2003.

56. Alison Langley, "World Health Meeting Approves Treaty to Discourage Smoking," *New York Times*, May 22, 2003, p. A11.

57. David Bollier, "The Rise of Netpolitik: How the Internet Is Changing International Politics and Diplomacy," Aspen Institute (2003), a report of the eleventh annual Aspen Institute Roundtable on Information Technology, available at: http://www.aspeninst.org/AspenInstitute/files/CCLIBRARYFILES/FILENAME/0000000077/netpolitik.pdf), pp. 21, 23, 24.

58. Ghana Cyber Group, Inc., "A Brief History of GCG" (July 28, 2003), available at: http://www.ghanacybergroup.com; see also "Net Effect: Africa's Expat Politics," *Foreign Policy*, September-October 2003, p. 51. I am indebted to Alexandra Scacco for calling my attention to this case.

59. Heather Timmons, "Shell to Avoid Oil Drilling at Sites Listed by UNESCO," *New York Times*, August 31, 2003, p. A8.

60. European Commission, Eurobarometer 56, October-November 2001, available at: http://europa.eu.int/comm/public_opinion/archives/eb_arch_en.htm).

61. Pew Global Attitudes Project, "Views of a Changing World June 2003" (Washington, D.C.: Pew Research Center for the People and Press, 2003), p. T129.

62. German Marshall Fund and Compagnia di San Paulo, Transatlantic Trends 2003, "Topline Data," "Survey Results—Topline Data," p. 24.

63. Gallup polls, August 1985 and May 1951, available through the iPoll database at the Roper Center for Public Opinion Research, University of Connecticut, Storrs, Conn.

64. See Benjamin and Simon, pp. 57–68; Paul Berman, "The Philosopher of Islamic Terror," *The New York Times Magazine*, March 23, 2003, p. 24.

65. Benjamin and Simon, *Age of Sacred Terror*, p. 187.

66. John Mintz, "Wahhabi Strain of Islam Faulted," *Washington Post*, June 27, 2003, p. 11; Benjamin and Simon, *Age of Sacred Terror*, p. 187.

67. Jane Perlez, "Saudis Quietly Promote Strict Islam in Indonesia," *New York Times*, July 5, 2003, p. A3.

CHAPTER 4:
WIELDING SOFT POWER

1. "The Limited Power of the Purse," *The Atlantic Monthly*, November 2003, p. 54. For a classic study, see Gary Hufbauer, Jeffrey J. Schott, and Kimberly Ann Elliott, *Economic Sanctions Reconsidered*, 2nd ed. (Washington, D.C.: Institute for International Economics, 1990).

2. I am indebted to Jane Holl Lute for sharing this insight in a presentation to the Aspen Strategy Group in August 2003.

3. Richard Pells, *Not like Us* (New York: Basic Books, 1997), pp. 31–32.

4. Harold Lasswell, cited in Philip M. Taylor, *British Propaganda in the 20th Century* (Edinburgh: Edinburgh University Press, 1999), p. 37.

5. Creel quoted in Emily Rosenberg, *Spreading the American Dream* (New York: Hill & Wang, 1982), p. 79.

6. Ibid., p. 100.

7. Eden quoted in Reinhold Wagnleitner, *Coca-Colonization and the Cold War* (Chapel Hill: University of North Carolina Press, 1994), p. 50.

8. Pells, *Not like Us*, p. 33.

9. Rosenberg, *Spreading the American Dream*, p. 208.

10. Ibid., pp. 209–11.

11. Pells, *Not like Us*, pp. xiii.

12. Rosenberg, *Spreading the American Dream*, pp. 215–17.

13. Terry Deibel and Walter Roberts, *Culture and Information: Two Foreign Policy Functions* (Beverly Hills: Sage Publications, 1976), pp. 14–15.

14. Wagnleitner, *Coca-Colonization*, p. 58.

15. Mary Niles Maack, "Books and Libraries as Instruments of Cultural Diplomacy in Francophone Africa During the Cold War," *Libraries and Culture* 36 (Winter 2001), p. 66.

16. Carnes Lord, "The Past and Future of Public Diplomacy," *Orbis*, Winter 1998, pp. 49–72.

17. Rosaleen Smyth, "Mapping US Public Diplomacy in the 21st Century," *Australian Journal of International Affairs* 55, no. 3 (2001), p. 429.

18. Leo Bogart, *Cool Words, Cold War* (Washington, D.C.: American University Press, 1995), pp. xvii, xxix.

19. Deibel and Roberts, *Culture and Information*, p. 23.

20. Bogart, *Cool Words, Cold War*, p. xxiv, and Leo Bogart, "History of the Department of State During the Clinton Presidency (1993–2001)," Of-

fice of the Historian, Bureau of Public Affairs, U.S. Department of State, available at: http://www.state.gov/r/pa/ho/pubs/8518.htm.

21. Anthony J. Blinken, "Winning the War of Ideas," in Alexander T. J. Lennon, ed., *The Battle for Hearts and Minds: Using Soft Power to Undermine Terrorist Networks* (Cambridge, Mass.: MIT Press, 2003), p. 287.

22. Stephen Johnson and Helle Dale, "How to Reinvigorate U.S. Public Diplomacy," Heritage Foundation Backgrounder no. 1645 (Washington D.C.: Heritage Foundation, 2003), available at: http://www.heritage.org/Research/NationalSecurity/bg1645.cfm, p. 4.

23. British Broadcasting Corporation, BBC World Service, Annual Report 2002–2003, "Review of World Service and Global News," available at: http://www.bbc.co.uk/info/report2003/pdf/worldservice.pdf, p. 4.

24. Sanford J. Ungar, "The Voice of America, Muffled," *Washington Post*, November 10, 2003, p. A25.

25. Fareed Zakaria, "The Rise of Illiberal Democracy," *Foreign Affairs*, November-December 1997, p. 22. See also Fareed Zakaria, *The Future of Freedom: Illiberal Democracy at Home and Abroad* (New York: Norton, 2003).

26. Christopher Ross, "Public Diplomacy Comes of Age," in *The Battle for Hearts and Minds* (Cambridge, Mass.: MIT Press, 2003), p. 252.

27. Herbert A. Simon, "Information 101: It's Not What You Know, It's How You Know It," *Journal for Quality and Participation*, July-August 1998, pp. 30–33.

28. John Arquilla and David Ronfeldt, *The Emergence of Neopolitik: Toward an American Information Strategy* (Santa Monica: RAND Corporation, 1999), p. 53.

29. Edward Kaufman, "A Broadcasting Strategy to Win Media Wars," in *The Battle for Hearts and Minds* (Cambridge, Mass.: MIT Press, 2003), p. 303

30. Matthew Collin, *Guerrilla Radio* (New York: Nation Books, 2001).

31. Murrow quoted in Mark Leonard, *Public Diplomacy* (London: Foreign Policy Centre, 2002), p. 1.

32. Leonard, *Public Diplomacy*, chapter 3.

33. Blinken, "Winning the War of Ideas," p. 291.

34. Hans N. Tuch, *Communicating with the World: U.S. Public Diplomacy Overseas* (New York: St. Martins Press, 1990), chapter 12.

35. Johnson and Dale, "How to Reinvigorate U.S. Public Diplomacy," p. 2.

36. Beers quoted in Leonard, *Public Diplomacy*, p. 19.

37. Butler quoted in ibid., p. 14.

38. Newt Gingrich, "Rogue State Department," *Foreign Policy*, July 2003, p. 42.

39. Senator Chuck Hagel, "Challenges of World Leadership," speech to the National Press Club, June 19, 2003.

40. Blinken, "Winning the War of Ideas," p. 289.

41. Leonard, *Public Diplomacy*, p. 53.

42. Keith Reinhard, "Restoring Brand America," *Advertising Age*, June 23, 2003, p. 30.

43. Truman quoted in Rosenberg, *Spreading the American Dream*, p. 216.

44. Frank A. Ninkovich, *The Diplomacy of Ideas: US Foreign Policy and Cultural Relations, 1938–1950* (Cambridge: Cambridge University Press, 1981), p. 176.

45. Dana Priest, "A Four Star Foreign Policy? U.S. Commanders Wield Rising Clout, Autonomy," *Washington Post*, September 28, 2000, p. A1; see also Dana Priest, *The Mission: Waging War and Keeping Peace with America's Military* (New York: Norton, 2003).

46. James Dao and Eric Schmitt, "Pentagon Readies Efforts to Sway Sentiment Abroad," *New York Times*, February 19, 2002, p. 1; Eric Schmitt, "Rumsfeld Says He May Drop New Office of Influence," *New York Times*, February 25, 2002, p. 13.

47. Deibel and Roberts, *Culture and Information*, p. 51.

48. Leonard, *Public Diplomacy*, chapter 3.

49. M. Kohut, "The Role of American Soft Power in the Democratization of Czechoslovakia," unpublished paper, Kennedy School of Government, April 2003.

50. Gates quoted in Daniel C. Thomas, *The Helsinki Effect: International Norms, Human Rights, and the Demise of Communism* (Princeton: Princeton University Press, 2001), p. 257.

51. Roula Khalaf and Gareth Smyth, "Arab World Held Back by Poor Governance," *Financial Times*, September 9, 2003.

52. "An Arab Reform Voice," *Washington Post*, November 7, 2003, p. A30.

53. United Nations Development Programme, "Arab Human Development Report 2002," available at: http://www.undp.org/rbas/ahdr/english.html.

54. William J. Burns, "Democratic Change and American Policy in the Middle East," remarks to the Center for the Study of Islam and Democracy, Washington, D.C., May 16, 2003.

55. Ambassador Edward Walker, "Policies for the Coming Decades: The Middle East," paper presented to the Aspen Strategy Group, August 2003.

56. Condoleezza Rice, "Middle East 'Transformation': Not So Simple," *Washington Post*, August 16, 2003, p. 20; see also President Bush's remarks on the twentieth anniversary of the National Endowment for Democracy, available at: http://www.whitehouse.gov/releases/2003/11/20031106-2.html.

57. Robert Satloff, "Re-engage the World," *Baltimore Sun*, March 9, 2003.

58. Danielle Pletka, quoted in Amy Cortese, "U.S. Reaches Out to Younger Readers, in Arabic," *New York Times*, February 17, 2003, p. C7.

59. Steven Weisman, "U.S. Must Counteract Image in Muslim World, Panel Says," *New York Times*, October 1, 2003, p. 1.

60. William Burns, "Democratic Change and American Policy in the Middle East"; see also Center for the Study of the Presidency, *Strengthening U.S.-Muslim Communications* (Washington, D.C.: Center for the Study of the Presidency, 2003).

61. James Sterngold, "Shah's Son Enlists Exiles in U.S. in Push to Change Iran," *New York Times*, December 3, 2001, p. A12.

62. Johnson and Dale, "How to Reinvigorate U.S. Public Diplomacy."

63. Newton Minow, "The Whisper of America," *Congressional Record* 147, no. 43 (April 17, 2002).

64. NAFSA: Association of International Educators, *In America's Interest: Welcoming International Students*, report of the Strategic Task Force on International Access, available at NAFSA website: http://www.nafsa.org/content/PublicPolicy/stf/inamericasinterestwelcomingInternational Students.pdf, p. 8.

65. Victor Johnson, Association of International Educators, quoted in Diana Jean Schemo, "Electronic Tracking System Monitors Foreign Students," *New York Times*, February 17, 2003, p. A11.

66. Council on Foreign Relations, "Public Diplomacy: A Strategy for Reform," report of an independent task force on public diplomacy, sponsored by the Council on Foreign Relations (New York: Council on Foreign

Relations, September 2002), available at: http://www.cfr.org/pubs/Task-force_final2-19.pdf.

67. Richard Pells, "American Historians Would Do Well to Get Out of the Country," *Chronicle of Higher Education*, June 20, 2003, p. B9.

Table 4.1. Public diplomacy spending figures from: U.S. Department of State "FY 2004 Budget in Brief" and "FY 2004 International Affairs (Function 150) Budget Request" (http://www.state.gov/m/rm/). France and Japan: Margaret Wyszomirski, Christopher Burgess, and Catherine Peila, "International Cultural Relations; A Multi-Country Comparison" (http://www.culturalpolicy.org/issuepages/Arts&Minds.cfm). U.K.: Wyszomirski (cited) and BBC World Services "Annual Report and Accounts 2002–2003." Germany: Goethe-Institut, "About Us" (http://www.goethe-institut.de/uun/enindex.htm). Defense spending figures from International Institute for Strategic Studies, *The Military Balance 2002–2003* (London: Oxford University Press, 2002), pp. 243–244, 252–255, 299.

CHAPTER 5:
SOFT POWER AND AMERICAN FOREIGN POLICY

1. Thomas Pickering, interviewed by Michelle Keleman, *Weekend Edition*, National Public Radio, Sunday, July 13, 2003.

2. Richard Bernstein, "Foreign Views of U.S. Darken After Sept 11," *New York Times*, September 11, 2003, p. 1

3. Paul Kelly, "Power Pact," *The Australian*, July 26, 2003, p. 1.

4. European Commission, Eurobarometer 59, available at: http://europa.eu.int/comm/public_opinion/archives/eb/eb59/eb59–en.htm, pp. B8, B36, B32, B33.

5. Pew Global Attitudes Project, *What the World Thinks in 2002* (Washington, D.C.: Pew Research Center for the People and the Press, 2002), p. T49.

6. Gallup International, "Post War Iraq 2003 poll," press release, May 13, 2003, available at: http://www.gallup-international.com; Pew Global Attitudes Project, *Views of a Changing World June 2003* (Washington, D.C.: Pew Research Center for the People and the Press, 2003), p. T132. Age demographics are available from the Pew Research Center on request (www.people-press.org).

7. *Newsweek* poll of 1983 compared to Pew Global Attitudes Project. The *Newsweek* data are from the iPoll database at the Roper Center for Public Opinion Research, University of Connecticut, Storrs, Conn. *Views of a Changing World June 2003* is available from Pew Research Center (www.people-press.org).

8. Wendy Melillo, "Ad Industry Doing Its Own Public Diplomacy," *Adweek*, July 21, 2003.

9. Fouad Ajami, "The Falseness of Anti-Americanism," *Foreign Policy*, September-October 2003, p. 61.

10. Cal Thomas, "Muzzling the Wrong Dog," *Washington Times*, October 23, 2003, p. 21. Thomas was defending the anti-Islamic statements of General William Boykin.

11. "Poll: One-third of Germans Believe US May Have Staged Sept. 11 Attacks," Reuters, July 23, 2003. See also "1 in 5 Germans Think It Was Maybe U.S.," *Chicago Sun-Times*, July 25, 2003, p. 6.

12. When Ambassador Jean-David Levitte of France pointed out a series of lies and false rumors circulating about French positions in 2003, few American newspapers carried his corrections. See Kim Housego, "France Calls for Fuller U.S. Response to Allegations of Disinformation Campaign," AP Online, May 16, 2003.

13. Office of the President, "National Security Strategy of the United States," available at: http://www.whitehouse.gov/nsc/nss.html.

14. John Lewis Gaddis, "Bush's Security Strategy," *Foreign Policy*, November-December 2002.

15. General John Abizaid, quoted in Eric Schmitt, "General in Iraq Says More G.I.s Are Not the Answer," *New York Times*, August 9, 2003, p. 1; Steven Weisman, "U.S. Set to Cede Part of Control over Aid for Iraq," *New York Times*, October 20, 2003, p. 1.

16. Max Boot, "America and the UN, Together Again?" *New York Times*, August 3, 2003; Charles Krauthammer, "Help Wanted," *Time*, September 1, 2003, p. 72.

17. Qingxin Ken Wang, "Hegemony and Socialisation of the Mass Public: The Case of Postwar Japan's Cooperation with the United States on China Policy," *Review of International Studies* 29 (2003), p. 119.

18. John Arquilla and David Ronfeldt, *The Emergence of Neopolitik: Toward an American Information Strategy* (Santa Monica: RAND Corporation, 1999), p. 52.

19. Robert Kaplan, "Islam vs. the West," interview, *Rolling Stone*, August 7, 2003, p. 38.

20. William Kristol, quoted in "A Classicist's Legacy: Empire Builders," *New York Times*, Week in Review, May 4, 2003.

21. Max Boot, "The Case for an American Empire," *The Weekly Standard*, October 15, 2001.

22. Andrew Bacevich, *American Empire: The Realities and Consequences of U.S. Diplomacy* (Cambridge, Mass.: Harvard University Press, 2002).

23. David Abernethy, *The Dynamics of Global Dominance: European Overseas Empires 1415–1980* (New Haven: Yale University Press, 2000), p. 19.

24. "U.S. Officials See Signs of a Revived Al Qaeda in Several Nations," *New York Times*, May 17, 2003, p.1

25. Fischer quoted in John Vinocur, "German Official Says Europe Must Be U.S. Friend, Not Rival," *New York Times*, July 19, 2003, p. A5.

26. Niall Ferguson, "The Empire Slinks Back," *New York Times Magazine*, April 27, 2003, p. 52.

27. Ernest May, *American Imperialism: A Speculative Essay* (Chicago: Imprint Publications, 1991).

28. Michael Ignatieff, "American Empire: The Burden," *New York Times Magazine*, January 5, 2003, p. 22.

29. Walter Russell Mead, *Special Providence: American Foreign Policy and How It Changed the World* (New York: Knopf, 2001).

30. Eric Schmitt, "Rumsfeld Says More G.I.'s Would Not Help U.S. in Iraq," *New York Times*, September 11, 2003.

31. Newt Gingrich, "Rogue State Department," *Foreign Policy*, July 2003, p. 42.

32. Juliette Antunes Sablosky, "Recent Trends in Department of State Support for Cultural Diplomacy: 1993–2002," available at Center for Arts and Culture website: http://www.culturalpolicy.org/pdf/JASpaper.pdf.

33. Michael Holtzman, "Washington's Sour Sales Pitch," *New York Times*, October 4, 2003.

34. Peter Slevin, "U.S. Pledges Not to Torture Terror Suspects," *Washington Post*, June 27, 2003, p. A1.

35. Philip Stephens, "The World Needs a Confident America, Not a Fearful One," *Financial Times*, December 12, 2002, p. 21.

36. Cathy Newman, "Blair Tells Congress 'Don't Give Up on Europe—Work with It,'" *Financial Times*, July 18, 2003, p. 1.

37. Richard Stevenson, "New Threats and Opportunities Redefine U.S. Interests in Africa," *New York Times*, July 7, 2003.

38. Gallup Poll, Ltd., "European Attitudes Toward the Gulf Crisis," October 1990. Gallup data are available through the iPoll database at the Roper Center for Public Opinion Research, University of Connecticut, Storrs, Conn.

Index

Attractiveness, x, 11, 12–13, 15, 26
  chemistry of, 5
  coercion and, 9
  cooperation and, 129
  culture and, 49, 68, 75, 96
  decline in, xii, 35–36, 44, 57–60,
    128–29, 147
  dimensions of, 33–34, 36, 42–43
  economic power and, 33
  enhancing, 6, 89
  foreign policy and, 60
  information age and, 133–34
  intangible, 7
  in Islamic world, 42 (fig.)
  modernity and, 43
  outcomes and, 18
  policies and, 35, 128
  politics and, 31
  power and, 6, 16, 31, 134
  repulsion and, 29, 150n8
  soft power and, 46, 63, 64, 74, 95, 145
  source of, 8, 134
  U.S., in Africa, 71 (fig.)
  U.S., in Americas, 72 (fig.)
  U.S., in Europe, 69 (fig.)
  U.S., in Southeast Asia, 70 (fig.)
  values and, 61
Audience, soft power and, 95
Aum Shinryko cult, 23
Axis of evil, 112

Bacevich, Andrew: on American empire,
  135
Balance of power, 4, 26, 45, 83
Ban the bomb movement, 35
Basque separatists, 24
Battle of Seattle (1999), 92
BBC, 50, 54, 67, 101, 104
Beatles, 40, 49, 50
Beckham, David, 40
Beers, Charlotte: on exchanges, 109–10
Behavior, 3, 14, 57
  acceptable, 20
  cultural resources and, 11
  influencing, 2, 7
  outcomes of, 6
  psy-ops and, 116
  types of, 7, 8

Berlin Wall, 49
Bilateralism, 146
Bill and Melinda Gates Foundation, 114
Bill of Rights, x, 79
Bin Laden, Osama, x, 2, 22
  Al Jazeera and, 108
  confidence in, 97
  fundamentalists and, 2
  hate speech of, 108
  recruitment by, 29, 44
  Saudi government and, 96
  soft power and, 130
  strong horse and, 26
  world affairs and, 97
Biological weapons, 24
Blair, Tony, 29, 97, 144
BMW, 128
B–92 radio station, 47, 106
Boeing, 82
Bollier, David, 92
Bollywood, 10, 33
Bolton, John: criticism of, 67
Books
  publication of, 34, 57
  sales of, 76, 85
Boot, Max, 133, 135, 138
Boston Symphony, 86
Bound to Lead (Nye), xi
Bové, Jose, 40
Boycotts, 44, 48, 55, 130
Brand names, 33, 76, 85
  multinational, 112
  selling off, 54–55
  soft power of, 90
Bremer, L. Paul, 133
Brent Spar drilling rig, 93
Britain, *See* Great Britain
British Council, 53, 109
British Empire, 136
British Tourist Authority, 109
Broadcasting, 111, 112, 113
Broadcasting Board of Governors, VOA
  and, 103–4, 123
Bulgaria, opinion of U.S., 56
Bureaucracy, 82, 89
Burns, William, 122
Bush, George H. W., 27, 67
  coalition building by, 145

PUBLICAFFAIRS is a publishing house founded in 1997. It is a tribute to the standards, values, and flair of three persons who have served as mentors to countless reporters, writers, editors, and book people of all kinds, including me.

I. F. STONE, proprietor of *I. F. Stone's Weekly*, combined a commitment to the First Amendment with entrepreneurial zeal and reporting skill and became one of the great independent journalists in American history. At the age of eighty, Izzy published *The Trial of Socrates*, which was a national bestseller. He wrote the book after he taught himself ancient Greek.

BENJAMIN C. BRADLEE was for nearly thirty years the charismatic editorial leader of *The Washington Post*. It was Ben who gave the *Post* the range and courage to pursue such historic issues as Watergate. He supported his reporters with a tenacity that made them fearless, and it is no accident that so many became authors of influential, best-selling books.

ROBERT L. BERNSTEIN, the chief executive of Random House for more than a quarter century, guided one of the nation's premier publishing houses. Bob was personally responsible for many books of political dissent and argument that challenged tyranny around the globe. He is also the founder and was the longtime chair of Human Rights Watch, one of the most respected human rights organizations in the world.

For fifty years, the banner of Public Affairs Press was carried by its owner, Morris B. Schnapper, who published Gandhi, Nasser, Toynbee, Truman, and about 1,500 other authors. In 1983 Schnapper was described by *The Washington Post* as "a redoubtable gadfly." His legacy will endure in the books to come.

Peter Osnos, *Publisher*